Promises To Keep

A CENTENNIAL HISTORY of CALVIN COLLEGE

JOHN J. TIMMERMAN

CALVIN COLLEGE AND SEMINARY with
WILLIAM B. EERDMANS PUBLISHING COMPANY

CONTENTS

PREFACE

Many readers skip prefaces. I think that is a mistake. A preface may indicate unexpected or undesired treatment of a subject, stimulate the merely curious, illuminate the author's intentions, and disclose the temper of the writer. I hope the readers of this book read its preface because the book's subject matter could be lengthily treated and its obvious shrinkage should be explained.

This history of Calvin College is primarily about people: their convictions, behavior, personalities, and achievements. Even the four shifts from a pastor's study to Knollcrest are recorded for the sake of their human impact. I have tried to portray the administration, faculty, and students as an interacting community in which all are important. Theological and philosophical ideas, so important a context of the college, are reviewed largely as they affected the attitudes and actions of the college community. Furthermore, I assume a general acquaintance with the college and the church that supports it. It would double the length of the book to make us wholly intelligible. This book tries to suggest what it was like to teach, study, and live in the Calvin community. Except for one chapter, little is said about the curriculum, an important and magnificent affair no doubt, but largely of genuine concern to experts only. Anyone trying to discover the details of the Pre-Law course in 1928 will be disappointed.

One of my friends said to me, "You don't expect many people to read this book do you?" So far my wife and I have read it; if anyone else reads it I shall be grateful. Whether anyone else reads it, the process of research and writing has been a pleasure. Stirring up old memories, dusty magazines, musty documents, and curious memorabilia was a happy task. Thinking about fine teachers and pleasant students was another. Re-creating bygone scenes and remembering old places constituted a third appeal. Though I did not like all I found, writing about it was a challenge. Samuel Daniel, the English poet, once said he enjoyed scholarship because "it me delights." Even though his play *The Vision of the Twelve Goddesses*

7

isn't as exciting as it sounds, Daniel enjoyed writing it. Much of the same is true here.

A writer of a book like this is bothered about what he should include about the people he describes. Many of them are still alive, and if they are not, their relatives are. Obviously, for instance, one cannot identify the professor who said to a colleague complaining about filling out a questionnaire concerning his activities, "Just tell them you talk a lot." Nor can one identify the characters in the following little scene. A professor fainted while working in the garden. Two of his neighbors rushed to help, and when they arrived at the back screen-door, his wife shouted, "Did you take his rubbers off?" One should not chronicle a mean or vindictive act completely out of character. Nor, on the other hand, should one assemble biographical accounts of pure sainthood, faultless, angelic beings cakewalking around with a halo. I have tried to be honest and fair, respecting the fact that some people are better than others.

A history of Calvin should have portraits of the characters who greatly affected her history. "An institution," says Emerson, "is the lengthened shadow of one man." Carlyle saw history as being made not by environment and event but by "event-making" men and women. I believe this is true of Calvin College. If one could have removed a dozen personalities from her history, it would have been enormously different. Their achievements should be recorded; but what about all the others, especially the other members of the Calvin faculty without whom they could have made no achievement at all? This has been a thorny problem to solve, particularly in the case of uncommonly gifted teachers whose visibility is largely limited to the classroom, and in the case of strikingly able younger faculty members whose contributions have not yet reached full stature. There are also many retirees who have done much for Calvin. Any sympathetic reader will realize I could not honor them all and still retain the design of this book. I have commented on faculty members who died while still in active service because their deaths greatly affected the Calvin community.

The chapter entitled "Latitudes Unknown," which includes the clamorous and crowded events from 1962 to 1974, proved the most difficult to write. I have tried to describe in uncomfortable proximity to them what seem to me the decisive events: the move to a new campus; student initiative together with administrative and faculty reaction; and the effect of both within and without the campus. I have devoted a separate chapter to the 4-1-4 curriculum, and I have described developments in chapel and the library elsewhere.

In writing this book I have not consciously followed or created an image of Calvin College. I have tried to tell the story as truly as my imperfect vision and loyalties permitted me to. The book has no footnotes, but it had many sources. I owe most to Dr. Henry Ryskamp's scholarly, unpublished history of Calvin College up to 1963 and to Dr. George Stob's penetrating and sprightly thesis *The Christian Reformed Church and Her Schools*. I have made a substantial use of the Calvin College *Chimes,* not because I regard it as either infallible or always representative but because it reflects the pulse of the day, often brilliantly. The *Prism* is a revealing pictorial history of the college. I owe a debt to the memories of my friends. Dean Vanden Berg kindly read my chapter on the 4-1-4, so I could be sure my own loyal opposition was kept within bounds. I am especially grateful to Dr. Herbert Brinks, curator of the Heritage Hall Historical Collection, for unusual encouragement and help.

I wish also publicly to thank my wife Carolyn for helpful suggestions, constant encouragement, and the transformation of my inept script into the immaculately typed pages of the manuscript.

Finally, I wish to thank the Centennial Observance Committee for encouragement and the freedom to treat the materials for this history in my own way.

—J.J.T.

Promises
To Keep

CHAPTER ONE

FORGOTTEN BENEFACTORS

When the Reverend Mr. Boer, officially appointed docent of the Theological School by the General Assembly of the True Holland Reformed Church on February 18, 1876, began teaching seven students everything in the curriculum, he did so on the second floor of an elementary school building on Williams Street, which crossed Commerce Avenue in a section of Grand Rapids not known for gentility. Train whistles pierced the air; the clatter and rumble of the big engines penetrated the classrooms, and swirls of smoke eddied about the windows. Here he taught his seven students Dutch, Latin, Greek, Hebrew, General History and Dutch History, Geography, Psychology, Logic, and Rhetoric. Since this apparently consumed but a fraction of his energy, he also taught Dogmatics, Hermeneutics, Exegetics, Isagogics, Church History, Symbolism, and Practical Theology. Of course it took him seven years to do this, but even at that it is an awesome regimen. It is no wonder that he preferred small textbooks and students who largely taught themselves. The motto given to the students in his inaugural address was *Per ardua ad astra.* This one man's multiversity was short-lived and Boer soon received valuable assistance.

How had the Reverend Mr. Boer, an able and intelligent man with a fine education, been persuaded into such an absurd situation? What were the basic attitudes and convictions of those who convinced him and whom he loyally served? Why did these attitudes come to exercise a permanent influence not only on the seminary but on the college to be developed years later? The answers to these questions help one understand the origin and progress of Calvin College.

Reverend Egbert Boer had accepted this extremely difficult, almost quixotic, task because of the great need for pastors in the small, struggling churches which had left the Reformed church in 1857. The new Holland Reformed Church had only two ministers at the time of secession, one of whom defected. In 1861 the church called itself the True Holland Reformed Church. It bore this singu-

larly challenging name until 1880, when it became the Holland Christian Reformed Church. To complete this little history of wobbly no-
menclature, I should add that it became the Christian Reformed
Church in 1890, a name retained ever since. (It has been modified
a bit by periodical defectors upon leaving.) The Holland Reformed
Church and its immediate successor tried energetically to recruit
ministers from the Netherlands, but since efforts were generally fruit-
less, the General Assembly (later Synod) decided to "prepare them
ourselves." At the 1863 meeting of the Assembly, Reverend W. H.
Van Leeuwen of Grand Rapids was appointed to prepare students
for the ministry. Thus began what was called "the school in the parsonage." Reverend Vander Werp served effectively later on and
Reverend Boer began his work in this fashion, but on March 15, 1876,
the birthday of Calvin Seminary and Calvin College, he made his inaugural address as docent of the Theological School, as it was then
known.

Reverend Mr. G. E. Boer had come from the Netherlands in
1875 to become pastor of the Spring Street True Holland Reformed
Church. He was magnetic in personality, popularly attractive in
preaching, a conciliatory leader, and a well of helpfulness. He was
also a man of great physical and nervous resources; he not only min-
istered to this large congregation but also edited *De Wachter*. Adding
the formidable curriculum to these duties was obviously impossible;
so he was appointed a full-time professor in February 1876, at $1300
a year, which at that time was a good salary. The range of subject
matter taught necessitated the appointment of another teacher. Reverend Boer was assisted by Geerhardus Vos in 1882-83, and by Reverend Mr. Hemkes, who served the seminary for many years as a
regular professor. Reverend Mr. Boer taught twenty-seven and Reverend Mr. Hemkes twenty-four hours a week. Even granting that
many of the subjects were on the high school level, that pupil-teacher
ratios were low, and that nobody expected rigorous scholarly standards, the burden was enormous. The burden was intensified by the
fact that many of the students were no longer young and pliable,
and were often unaccustomed to sustained study. Many came to the
intricacies of Greek verbs from weeding cabbages, picking corn, or
delivering milk cans. The little textbooks saved time, but they also
gave concise surveys of the entire field. The variety of texts and
courses doubtless forced the student to independent study. There was
little time for coddling and counseling. The hard teaching loads
demanded alleviation, and in 1886 Geerhardus Vos was chosen as

docent. This was a memorably significant appointment, since Vos was a man of formidable intellectual gifts, an eminent scholar and teacher together.

Geerhardus Vos entered the Theological School in 1881, after having had an excellent training in the classical languages in the Netherlands. In 1882 he was appointed assistant to Docent Boer. After attending Princeton Seminary from 1883 to 1886, he attended the University of Strassburg, where he received his Ph.D. In September 1888 he returned to teach in the seminary. His appointment was signally important at the time. He introduced the students to the best theological scholarship of the day, to inquiry and study beyond mere perpetuation of tradition; he taught in the English language and thereby helped make possible witness in the language of the land; he greatly stimulated many able clergymen; his was the first impressive scholarship at the school and thereby stimulated appreciation for its importance.

Dr. Vos was a brilliant scholar and teacher whose impact on the minds of his students proved to be permanent. His mimeographed notes were abiding treasures to his students. My father kept and used them for years, and when he died in 1946, a theological professor from the University of Potchefstroom, South Africa, was more eager to obtain them than any other book in his library. This estimation was widespread, and when Vos refused his first appointment to Princeton there was joy in the school and church. However, in 1893 he accepted an appointment at Princeton, where he served with renown.

In 1878 the curriculum consisted of four years of literary studies, largely linguistic, and two years of seminary. The teaching methods were catechetical. The students recited, often in rote fashion, the exact words of the text. There was no opportunity for discussion in which, in the phrase of the sixties, the student could "do his own thing." In the words of "A Tree of Life," a pageant written by Henry Zylstra, the instruction in the manse and later in the seminary proceeded something like this:

Docent: What is the true church?
Student: The True Church is the communion of the elect, called to the fellowship of Christ.
Docent: How can you prove this?
Student: I Peter 2:9: . . . You are a chosen generation, a royal priesthood, a peculiar people.

This does sound dull indeed, but possibly remembering Pope's line, they might have replied, "Dulness is sacred in a sound divine." Later, in the notes of Dr. Vos, the material was more sophisticated and scholarly, but there was still an unusual emphasis upon the memory. Today many teachers and students would consider such emphasis archaic and useless. The pendulum is seldom at center; then the student memorized too much without mediating his materials, now he often reflects without knowing anything. At any rate, if one examines the graduates of the Theological School in the 1880's and 1890's, one is struck by their general competence, even eminence in some cases. These men when they added reflection to memory, as many of them did, mastered and retained an important body of theological as well as other knowledge. When they began "rapping," they did it with cudgels.

The Theological School, which included the Literary Department, was incorporated under the laws of Michigan in 1878. The Board of Trustees, known for many years as the Curatorium, was elected the same year. By 1883 there were thirty-six students in the Literary Department and fifteen in the seminary, with a faculty of four full-time and three part-time teachers. By the year 1900, ninety-four clergymen had been graduated. The Literary Department, whose admission policies were liberalized in 1894, was firmly established by the same year. The institution was supported by the Christian Reformed Church, composed in 1900 of 144 churches and 17,584 communicant members. The assessment for the institution was sixty cents per family.

The new institution faced grave problems from buildings to basic principles. To understand the subsequent character and life of Calvin College, it is necessary to look at the divided and sometimes divisive attitudes among its supporters. These attitudes are woven into the very texture of the history of the institution. Since, despite the adage about Johns Hopkins and the log, no college can function without proper buildings, let us first examine the early attempts to provide adequate facilities, a dramatic and recurring problem as Calvin moved from site to site.

Prior to 1876 theological instruction had been given in the manse and the prospective candidates moved with the pastor when he accepted a call. By 1876 this arrangement proved increasingly unsatisfactory, and when Docent Boer formally opened the school year in 1876, the school was located at 43 Williams Street, S.W., a block west of Division Avenue. The school was then white, neat, and ample.

The Christian elementary school occupied the first floor and the seminary the second. In those days graduates of the elementary school went directly to the Theological School for their preparatory years. Close by was the church building. This physical proximity suggested a symbolic closeness as well. A commemorative piece in *Chimes* quotes the following lines, source unknown:

> *It fears no skeptic's puny hands*
> *While near the school the church spire stands;*
> *Nor fears the blinded bigot's rule*
> *While near the church spire stands the school.*

Already by 1886 a slow decay was creeping over the neighborhood between the old Union Station and Division Avenue, so that in the same year Classis Holland proposed to Synod that the Theological School be moved to Holland, Michigan. The proposal lost by only three votes. The school moved instead to Franklin and Madison in

Williams Street Christian School.

1892. In 1926 the building on Williams Street, now grimy and shabby, with constantly falling shingles and almost impenetrably dusty windows, was occupied by the Salvation Army, where it parcelled out old clothes and furniture. On the second floor there stood a long table loaded with musty books still attracting an occasional theological student out for a bargain. Today, the site has become a dusty, unpaved parking lot; next to this are seedy quarters for bingo, held Wednesday through Friday from 7:30 to 10:30. Directly east across the street is a weed-grown lot filled with old tires and chunks of broken cement. Directly north, across the street, is the Mel Trotter Mission heralding its invitation, "Holding forth the word of life."

The upper rooms on Williams Street had become intolerably cramped by 1889, so in 1890 the property on Franklin and Madison was purchased. The Board of Trustees and Synod wished to build but had no money. The Reverend J. Noordewier, who had enthusiastically supported the project, found to his consternation that he had been appointed to raise the funds necessary. This was for him a disturbing request, since he was an ordained clergyman serving an attractive congregation in the idyllic village of Fremont. In those days ministerial dignity was at its peak; now he was asked to go from church to church in the United States and beg for money. But his devotion to the cause prevailed and he received four months' leave of absence from his congregation. There were over ninety congregations to visit by train, some very slow, and by horse-and-buggy. He was then urged to leave Fremont and continue solicitations as a home missionary of the church. He continued this work from 1891 to 1893. The completed building cost more than expected, as buildings almost always do, but when it was dedicated in 1892, the debt was only a little over $5,000. Noordewier's achievement was notable, typical, and sacrificial. He gave up a pleasant charge, raised a large sum of money in small amounts from people of humble means, often suffering indignities while so doing. Calvin College throughout its years has owed an enormous debt to the idealistic generosity of many others, largely anonymous, who were similarly motivated.

The new building, familiar to most of us as the old Christian High School building, was dedicated in 1892. It seemed almost extravagantly ample to the forty students and three teachers who were to occupy it. There were seven spacious classrooms, each capable of holding the entire student body, an auditorium able to hold the students five times over, a library room, a small laboratory, and a few other small rooms. In two decades it was too small, and the vision that produced it had again to be enlarged. Providentially it made possible, however, the immediate execution of the dramatic decision about liberalized admissions in 1894.

The Theological School was established because of an acute need for an educated clergy. Soon a similar need was felt for properly educated teachers in the Christian Schools that were slowly rising, often in the face of hard opposition even in the church. In 1883 there were three such schools in Grand Rapids, and in 1894 twenty Christian schools in the denomination. Their supporters were profoundly concerned about the commitment and proper education of teachers for these schools. Where would the graduates of elementary schools pursue their further education? The Literary Department of the Theological School seemed to suggest an answer. Dr. Henry Zwaanstra, in his fine book *Reformed Thought and Experience in a New World,* says, "Boer first suggested separating the literary from the theological department of the Theological School." The Reverend Mr. B. K. Kuiper said that a college had to come. By separating the Literary Department, by widening its curricula, and by establishing a college, some leaders thought covenant youth would receive proper preparation for Christian school teaching. They would become acquainted with Reformed perspectives as they applied to teaching and they would be spared the unsettling influences of the American public schools and colleges. Calvinism always drives to unified perspectives and consistently unified action. Whatever segment of education it begins with, it will implicitly drive full circle. Such leaders as J. Vander Mey, H. Beets, K. Schoolland, and B. K. Kuiper saw the need and pressed for this solution. The first fruits of such convictions were realized in the historic decision of 1894, although the adoption of a normal school or Department of Education was not enthusiastically endorsed by the college itself during the first decades of the new century. The destiny of the Theological School, college, and normal school were, however, interlocked, and all three depended on the support of a constituency interestingly divided in attitude.

Both the Theological School and later the college were supported by a constituency with a divided mind about the proper nature of education on whatever level. One group was primarily concerned with education, if it were really necessary at all, as a kind of carekeeping, an unsullied, unaltered transmission of received truths. The other group had a different mind. No less concerned about the perpetuation of confessional truth, it was also interested in developing it.

The faith once delivered could be quarried for new insight, strengthened and enriched by the studying of other views. The former group
had little concern with the world of culture; the latter wished to
influence, even reform it.

These perspectives arose in the Netherlands and were fostered
and tempered by American experience. In 1834 a small group of
Dutch and German separatists broke with the Dutch Reformed
Church in a movement known as *De Afscheiding*. The separatists
were convinced that the state church in its rationalism denied the
depravity of the human heart and the absolute necessity of conver-
sion, and that its way of life was worldly and often impious. Their
genuine piety insisted upon a close, self-denying walk with God,
marked by unceasing gratitude for His grace and a strong desire
to remain unspotted by the world. Ordinary people, trying to move
through Vanity Fair with a minimum involvement in its gauds, shows,
and treasures, they were convinced in their bones of the reality of
the antithesis, and they meant to keep themselves and their children
safe in the Lord. Many were also deeply interested in theology and
read widely in the early Reformed theologians. They were also ec-
clesiastically very self-centered, and this interest both in themselves
and their descendants sometimes concerned itself with bitter disputes
about trivia, which sometimes identified parochial habit with divine
command. It was in many ways a fierce faith, and when they came
to a huge, alien, and bewildering land with its raucous materialism
and wide variety of religions, these tendencies were often intensified,
and they took heroic and sacrificial measures to insure the perpetuity
of God's peculiar people.

Years later in the 1880's a second secession of a very different
nature occurred in the Netherlands. This movement was known as
the *Doleantie* and its membership included many cultivated people.
Its leader was Abraham Kuyper, a versatile genius who served not
only his own followers in an amazing variety of ways but the Dutch
nation as statesman and prime minister. Kuyper was no separatist in
the early sense; he believed in involvement with and transformation
of the world about him. He wished to give Christ preeminence in
all walks of life: the shop and the factory; the home and school;
the church and the state; the arts and the life of the mind. He affirmed the reality of common grace, whereby the non-Christian
world produces good things which the Christian may appropriate
and transform to the glory of God. The Reformed Christian should
not retreat into culturally impoverished ghettoes but should enter

the world not only to sow the good seed of the gospel but to enrich its life through cultural contributions. Education moulds students into a leaven. The Christian is being truly grateful when he illuminates learning through his beliefs and shares the truth with others. It is but fair to add, I think, that at first the main interest of American followers of Kuyper was theological; only through steady and persuasive leadership did their interests extend to other areas of life.

Which emphasis is right? Is God best served by fleeing a lost world, meditating on the blessings of special grace, and restricting one's life as far as possible to familial and ecclesiastical interests? Should one fashion schools on this basis? Will not exposure to the subtle and magnetic creations of the world attenuate one's allegiance to Christ, diminish wholehearted commitment, and lead to self-deceiving compromise? These were real and agonizing problems for many of our ancestors. They saw in worldly culture a threat and were inclined to a policy of quarantine. Should a loyal Christian demonstrate that loyalty by confronting opposing cultures, appropriating the truth they offer, and after studying them from the inside, assess them with a scholarly Christian perspective? Should one fashion schools which seek to understand, appreciate wherever possible, and confront when necessary opposing outlooks and sensibilities?

Profoundly sincere and serious men and women have struggled with these questions during Calvin's history. I don't suppose a Christian can ever lose sympathy with the mind of the Afscheiding; neither would he refuse to admit a risk in the other view. St. Paul says, "But we have the mind of Christ that we have received, not the spirit of the world, but the spirit which is of God." In the course of its development the supporters and teachers at Calvin have sought to make this statement come true in their college. The "mind of Christ" is the mind they have tried to think with, to understand and to judge with. The continuing hard intellectual effort at Calvin has been to nurture this mind, and the peril has been to lose it—to pragmatism, skepticism, materialism. The key words in Calvin's history, as I see it, have been *antithesis, integration, commitment,* and *involvement.* All suggest struggle and all connote the danger of a spiritual dichotomy in which one says that faith is important in church and in the study of literature and philosophy, but of less use in our pragmatic daily lives and in certain subjects where direct relationships are hard to see or emphasize. To make the mind of Christ lie "at the bottom of things" is an arduous task in which with our hardest efforts we but inch ahead.

The Theological School was but one of the pioneering adventures of the Christian Reformed Church, an adventure not of the spade against the soil or the ax against the tree, but no less herculean. One sees the Reverend Mr. C. Bode riding behind his broncos on the rugged roads of early Iowa, trying to organize new churches. During his career he was involved in organizing fourteen new churches, often traveling to them in a passenger car hooked onto a freight train. Similar heroic efforts were made in the Dakotas and Minnesota. In the years 1857-1893, when the Literary Department was opened to nontheological students, the church's missionary endeavors were inaugurated. The *Banner of Truth*, begun in 1866, was entrusted in 1893 to the editorship of the Reverend Mr. Henry Beets, a man who used its pages eloquently to champion the cause of the Literary Department. Social and ecclesiastical problems troubled the early pioneers, but in the eighties there was evident an increasing unity and tolerance so that these early efforts could flower. The settlers had begun to learn how to Americanize themselves without losing their heritage. Gradually, they began to enter American academic life. In 1894, Synod took a major step toward attracting its own youth to its institution and instituted a change which would transform the small school of fifty-one students and four faculty members into an ever growing institution which increasingly mobilized the best vision, courage, and idealism its supporters through the grace of God could summon.

Although not all were idealistic and some were stingy and others quarrelsome, the makers of the tradition that built Calvin College transmitted sturdy moral as well as intellectual values, stamina as well as insight. It was an heroic tradition in which courage was common, and endurance a necessity. Sod huts, blazing sun, and bitter cold in South Dakota. Lush crops but also drought, hail, and obliterating tornadoes in Iowa. The Reverend Mr. Van Raalte praying for parishioners dying of swamp fever. A lonely grave on a lonely trail between Holland and Grand Haven. Long hours in the acid smells of the silk mills of Paterson. Contempt from supercilious Americans who regarded them as narrow-minded bigots. Native acumen and industry brought them to wealth and the hazards of worldliness. The hard blows of outer and inner weather were always present; yet, through fierce and unquenched faith, through God's grace they created ultimately a system of reputable education from the kindergarten through the seminary.

Only a few years ago, the past was being dismissed as a bucket of ashes over which only a sentimentalist would grieve. Fortunately, the mood is changing and intelligence is replacing short-sighted feelings. The past is inescapably present even in those who repudiate it. Calvin College has had a quiet history and most of the violence has been verbal—no nonnegotiable demands, no mob violence, no dire confrontations. It is a moderately small college based on a deeply felt ideal and sacrificially supported over many years, one of the private colleges whose continuance is essential in a pluralistic society. This ideal has been stated at many times and in many ways. It is good to hear a student state it in the 1954 *Prism:*

> But the greatest idea about Calvin College is an intangible and an invisible one. It is the idea on which Calvin College was founded in 1876 and the idea on which it still exists in 1954. That idea is a dynamic faith in a living God.

This dynamic faith in a living God revealed in Scripture gripped the founders of the institution. The quiet heroism of preachers and pioneers, enduring privation most uncommon among us, building big when bricks were few, the struggle and the triumph, causes one to say when one remembers it all: "Blessed are the dead who die in the Lord from henceforth; Yea, saith the Spirit, that they may rest from their labors: for their works follow them."

CHAPTER TWO

GREAT EXPECTATIONS

Samuel Morison and Henry Steel Commager call the year 1894 "the darkest that Americans had known for thirty years." The panic of 1893 had reduced great railroads like the Santa Fe and the Union Pacific to failure; every week three or four banks were going bankrupt. Four million Americans were jobless; the unemployed rode the freights from town to unwelcoming town, and the hobo camps on the edge of cities terrified the citizens; the corn crop failed and the government in Washington seemed devoted only to the arrogant and well-heeled. Radicalism was in the air, but despite William Jennings Bryan's fervent campaign against the money standard and "soulless" capitalism, the country voted McKinley in as president in 1896 and most of the Dutch immigrants helped, though they also suffered greatly. It was during these dark days that Calvin College as an institution distinct from the Theological School was born.

On June 15, 1894, the Synod of the Christian Reformed Church adopted a momentous resolution. It deserves recording as it was passed:

> Om bij het reglement voor de Theologische School het volgende te voegen: 'ook zij die niet wenschen opgeleid te worden tot bedienaars des Woords, kunnen na een voldoend admissie examen, tot het Litt. gedeelte worden toegelaten.

> To add the following to the regulation for the Theological School: also those who do not wish to be prepared for the ministry, may be admitted to studies in the Literary Department after satisfactorily passing entrance examination.

This terse resolution opened the way to the making of Calvin College. Behind its adoption was the persuasive power and pressure of three large classes: Iowa, Holland, and Illinois. Their wish, however, that the Literary Department be separated from the theological department was denied. Two instructors, A. J. Rooks and G. Berkhof, were appointed to serve. Klaas Schoolland was appointed when G.

24

Berkhof died in November of 1894. All teachers in the school, still known as the Theological School, were called professors in the first catalog, published in 1896. It is interesting to note that the seminary professors were to receive $1300 a year, whereas the college teachers received $800, a bit of classical and clerical discrimination which, as it continued, later occasioned one resignation from the college and an outspoken petition by fourteen disgruntled scholars on the college faculty who knew they taught more hours and students, thought they were equally educated, and did not view the Theological School as a graduate but rather as a professional school. There was also at the time of the adoption of the resolution resentment among parents in regard to the church's subsidizing of children not their own, particularly those of Grand Rapids. Slowly swinging into focus also was the question whether it was any business of the church to support and control a college.

Dean A. J. Rooks in writing about the founding of the college in the *Semi-Annual Volume* begins his brief chapter with two quotations from "Cicero of Old." In the conclusion of the chapter he favors us with two more Latin quotations and in the middle of his history includes a crucially important, untranslated Dutch quotation. This was not pedantry or an ebullient flourish of his love of Latin. He simply assumed in 1926 when he wrote it that his readers would understand them. The students in the early college would have had no trouble at all; the number of college graduates who could do so in 1976 would be few, indicating how drastically the tools and ends of learning have altered.

Prior to the fall of 1894, only pre-seminary students had been admitted to the literary course, a four-year program dominated by the study of languages. It was a truly formidable curriculum, consisting of half a dozen languages together with such "breathers" as Philosophy or Logic. Granted that many of the students were older and more serious than high school students of today, it is still an astonishingly rigorous program to undertake after an elementary education, and one is impressed by the intellectual caliber of the survivors, who had to pass an oral examination on the entire program at the end of four years. One must add to the difficulties that some students worked to pay their keep, and that others did not spend their summers in review but in various hard tasks. My father travelled from farm to farm and little town to little town in Iowa and Illinois selling books to find means of support during the school year.

During the Great Depression of the early thirties, I knew some students whose main menu was peanuts, bread, and milk, but some of these earlier students had a spartan life also. Reverend Mr. J. J. Hiemenga in his interesting autobiography recalls that he rented a room for seventy-five cents a week, received clothes from a haberdasher in Zeeland for seven years, and free shoes from a shopkeeper there. He worked in a barber shop on Saturday afternoons and weekday evenings for seven warm meals a week. Later on for a time he enjoyed molasses, lard, and cold water for breakfast each day; in the evening he glutted himself in bread and sometimes a slice of bologna. This was too much. Finally, he discovered a place where he could get seven warm meals a week for a dollar. This case was not atypical. In 1974 students made disparaging remarks about meals in the Commons, whose menu would have proved a series of banquets to these early students.

Today a vexing problem at Calvin concerns transportation: the problems of parking or the lack of buses. In the early years of the century most students walked, though Principal Rooks frequently came by horse and buggy. There were, of course, streetcars, but they cost fifty cents a week. Some students walked from Alpine Avenue and beyond from the West side; others from Grandville Avenue and beyond in the Southwest. Students from other cities came to Calvin by coach; students from Iowa or Paterson sometimes came packed in tin-lizzies.

Although nontheological students had in 1894 been permitted to enter the Literary Department, there was no rush. In 1894 there were thirty-three students in this department; it dropped to twenty-nine in 1895 and then gradually rose till it had doubled in 1901. Both the depression and the linguistic requirements discouraged attendance. In fact, the curriculum was wholly designed for pre-seminary students, and Dean Rooks states that all students enrolled between 1894 and 1900 intended to enter the ministry. There were two main reasons for the dramatic increase in 1901.

Times improved slightly in 1900. The manual workingmen, who made up the bulk of the denomination, were less pinched. In the Grand Rapids area they worked long hours, rising at 5:30 a.m. to walk to a working day of ten hours, six days a week. A dollar a day was not unusual, but you could buy a good house for $600. Woodcarvers earned the most; skilled tradesmen made twenty-six cents an hour. When the furniture workers struck in Grand Rapids years later, they were supported by the Reverend John Groen. They wanted sixty hours' pay for a fifty-five hour week. Out of these means they were paying a quota of fifty-five cents per year toward the school. There were in 1900, 10,614 families in the Christian Reformed Church. Many supported local Christian schools as well as the Theological School. They had enough idealism and economic resources to support a growingly expensive institution.

Probably the main reason for the increased enrollment in the Literary Department in 1901 lay in a significant resolution approved in June of 1900 by the Synod. Although the resolution was directly concerned with the high school, the enlarged curriculum was also adopted, as Professor J. G. Vanden Bosch says, "with a view of expanding ultimately into a college." Here is the resolution:

(a) The Literary Department be extended to an Academy with a curriculum of four years followed by a transition year for students who wish to study Theology, whereas the Academy be opened for study for other purposes. The Academy course of four years is then to be in general preparatory while the transition year is chiefly for special preparation for the Seminary.

(b) The Synod resolve that two professors be appointed for the Academy so that henceforth there will be four teachers in the Literary Department.

The curriculum was further modified to appeal to students who might wish to continue their studies at college or to prepare for county or state teachers' examinations. A fifth year was added to the academy; though ostensibly in preparation for the seminary, it was actually the beginning of the college. Two professors who were to play a large role in Calvin's early history were appointed: J. G. Vanden Bosch and B. K. Kuiper, both picturesque and interesting figures in the history of the school.

Prospective students could now enroll in a theological preparatory course, a classical course, and a Latin-scientific course. The linguistic emphasis was still strong in all courses. Dr. J. P. Van Haitsma remembered that he took a "course in Philosophy with a Dutch-speaking Professor who used a German text when I was only seventeen." There were no soft spots in the curriculum, though there may have been in the professors.

Dr. George Stob, in his highly readable, penetrating, and delightfully independent work *The Christian Reformed Church and Her Schools,* says, "The year 1900 was the beginning of an era." That is true; it was the era of slow and deliberate growth of the Literary

Department into a college. The Synodical resolution of 1900 had inaugurated the era and the full-fledged college of 1920 completed it. In 1901 the institution celebrated its twenty-fifth anniversary with a faculty of ten and a student body of seventy-two. Eighty-four clergymen had been graduated from the Theological School. In 1902 the academy was accredited by the University of Michigan. Talk of a college was in the air. Campaigns to raise money were planned. Klaas Schoolland, says Stob, "wrote another series of learned articles about the necessity of a college, which nobody understood." Klaas Kuiper said bluntly, "We must have a college." There were great expectations but slow realizations. The growth was deliberate and carefully planned. There were no counterfeit claims or any really false starts. In 1904 it was decided to work toward a junior college, but the planning subsided when the money was scarce. In 1906, after a sum of $31,000 had been raised, Synod adopted the Board's proposal to add a second college year, and in the fall of 1907 students were able to enroll in the John Calvin Junior College. The salaries of the college teachers were raised to $1100 and those of the seminary to $1400. J. Broene and J. P. Van Haitsma were added to the faculty. In 1910 a third year of college was added, and Calvin's work began to draw notice.

The September 2, 1911, issue of *The Grand Rapids Press* carries a highly complimentary article on Calvin, then attended by 250 students. The *Press* praises the "standard of its faculty, the excellence of its instruction, and the achievement of its students." Discipline cases, it notes, are extremely rare. Calvin "challenges any college in the country to produce a better percentage of chapel attendance." Calvin's classical course is praised, and it notes that a Calvin student won the highest prize in the entrance examination at the University of Michigan. Mr. S. Ranck, city librarian, praises "the splendid work now being done by Calvin College." A student, we should remember, could enjoy all this, including the "very capable faculty," for twenty-six dollars a year.

Calvin began, as did many another private American college, out of a deeply felt need for an educated clergy. To insure an ever better preparation, its founders strengthened the academy and developed the college. To serve a greater variety of students, they liberalized both the policies of admission and the curriculum. That curriculum, though rather one-sided, was far from illiberal. All three phases of the institution were operating on the same premises, and even though the seminarians attended in the afternoon, they were not

COURSES OF STUDY.

THE COLLEGE.

FIRST YEAR.

Seminary Preparatory	Classical	Modern Classical
Latin 4 Greek 3 German 4 English 3 History 3 Public Speaking 1 Bible Study 1	Latin 4 Greek 3 German 4 English 3 History of Education 3 Bible Study 1	Latin 4 Chemistry 4 German 3 English 3 History of Education 3 Bible 1

SECOND YEAR.

Latin 3 Greek 3 German 4 History 3 Psychology and Logic } 3 Dutch 2	Latin 3 Greek or Mathematics } 3 German 4 Psychology and Logic } 3 Sociology 2 History 3	Latin or Mathematics } 3 German 3 French 3 History 3 Psychology and Logic } 3 Sociology 2

THIRD YEAR.

Latin 3 Greek 3 Hebrew 3 English 3 Dutch 2 Hist. of Philosophy 3 Public Speaking 1	Latin 3 Greek or Mathematics } 3 English 3 History 3 Hist. of Philosophy 3 Political Economy 2 Public Speaking 1	Latin or Mathematics } 3 English 3 French 3 History 3 Hist. of Philosophy 3 Political Economy 2 Public Speaking 1

College curriculum 1913.

invisible during the rest of the day. Therein lay a knot of problems.

Little boys in kneepants and long-haired girls in long skirts, first admitted in 1901, bubbling with youth and mischief, jostled staid and black-suited seminarians in the library and halls. Boys from lonely farms, whose overalls were then no badge of distinction, city boys from Chicago and Paterson, worldly-wise in their own eyes, and the larger Grand Rapids groups revealed a wide range of interests and preparation. Dean Rooks presided over this motley group, and in an early fall chapel, after welcoming the largest freshman class in years, read, inadvertently or not, Psalm 3, "Lord, how are they increased that trouble me. Many are they that rise up against me." He had no reason to retract these prophetic words. The young students trampled "the young shoots of the grass" in spring; they put a cat in a professor's desk, who in his anger hurled it out of a second-story window; they played pranks without ceasing. One group became so famous for its subversive activities that, to quote Dr. Pousma, it was hailed as "the Terrible Four, Ed, John, Kep and Van Goor." The underground was active, but the classes were kept in good form and education went on in the classrooms.

If it was busy inside, it was also busy outside. For years streetcars rattled and clanged by, and in warm days with open windows all sounds burst indoors. If there were a silent moment, the fire department, a block down, went out for exercise. I taught in this corner years later; it was noisier than ever because by that time the radiator system had become arthritic, and it hissed and detonated all through a winter's day. One of the unexpected pleasures of teaching on that corner was to see Dr. Henry Beets pace briskly from his house across the street and thumb a ride downtown to get his exercise at the Y.M.C.A. The man who for years was always in the car with visiting dignitaries to Grand Rapids had no false pride. Knowing Dr. Beets, I am sure that the former Director of Missions did not forget his missionary zeal as he rode to town.

As enrollment grew and the problems of housing such a varied student body in one building intensified, the building which was once considered palatial became cramped. In 1915 the preparatory school numbered 236, the junior college 61, and the seminary 44. Dean Rooks sparkles with joy when he writes about the new building a mile east on Franklin. The old building was sold to the newly formed Grand Rapids Christian School Association for $20,000 in 1920. Later it was razed to make room for a splendid high school building, which, in turn, was sold together with the other architecturally outstanding buildings to the Kent County Department of Social Services, a sale full of surprise, irony, and satisfaction.

A new site had already been considered early in the century. Dr. Beets, whose interest in the college was impressively demonstrated by his writing in *The Banner* and his service on the Board, had already in 1906 urged that the school obtain "at least twenty acres"

Calvin College 1917.

in the "suburbs of our city." He wanted the institution to obtain a
"large plot of ground at a suitable place." From 1906 to 1908 offers
for a future site were made by the city of Kalamazoo, which proposed the property of the Michigan Female Seminary for a very
reasonable price; by the Chamber of Commerce of Muskegon, which
offered the college ten acres and $10,000; and by the Board of Trade
of Grand Rapids, which promised $10,000 toward the project, a
sum never fully realized and largely collected by representatives of
the college. Expansion at the local site was rejected as too costly,
one of the reasons also given for moving to Knollcrest years later.
The Board of Trustees appointed a committee which in June 1909
purchased the new Franklin site for $12,000. The Administration
Building on the new site was erected at a cost of $150,000. The
site itself was located in what Dean Rooks called "the most desirable
and valuable section of the city of Grand Rapids." He describes the
main building with rare delight and he is greatly impressed by the
fact that "all around it are residences of the better class." At one
corner, he says, "lies Franklin Park, a twenty-acre plot of ground
offering splendid opportunity for rest and recreation." The *Kolonie*
had arrived. The cornerstone was laid on June 22, 1916.

There was great pride in the building of red brick set in white
mortar, its gleaming white cupola set on contrasting slate, the four

heavy pillars at the entrance with Corinthian floral tops— even "the smokestack could be seen for miles around." The basement had fifteen rooms, the first floor nineteen, and the second floor ten. The chapel seated 700. The people of Grand Rapids had contributed $50,000 in addition to the $11,000 largely collected by A. J. Rooks through the Board of Trade. On the dedicatory evening, September 4, 1917, the building was practically completed. The campus, however, was bare of bush or tree, a flat piece of sandy soil covered by grass. Over the years exquisite shrubs and beautiful trees were added.

Speeches seem to have been popular in those days. The audience was treated to an historical survey by B. K. Kuiper. Reverend Mr. J. Manni, speaking in the Dutch language, stressed the divine favors experienced by the school, repeating in large part what Kuiper had already recounted. Professor Heyns then spoke, after which A. J. Rooks expressed his gratitude. The chorus then interrupted, and Mr. Ralph Stob concluded the speeches. What strikes one in all the remarks is the genuine gratitude and pride that moved all the speakers. There was a huge crowd in celebration. It was a milestone, a real happening for the supporters of Calvin.

During these years A. J. Rooks, for many years Dean of Calvin College, served as Principal of the Literary Department. He was a kindly, genial man, with a resonant voice and accent, generally beloved by students and sometimes taken advantage of both in his teaching of Latin and his deanship. He performed a multitude of tasks: "making schedules of recitations and examinations, arranging courses of study, classification of students, minor infractions of discipline, and other duties, including acting for the President when absent or temporarily incapacitated." More than one student has heard him say "Would you like your 'fether' (father) to know about this?" During the years of the First World War, students who worked on the farm could skip the war. Here is a typical note to the dean:

Prof. Rooks:
Please give me consent to go and work on the farm. Have been brought up on the farme [sic]. Am intend to work home in Borculo.

These notes invariably appeared late in the second semester *just* before the final examinations upon the whole year's work. The examinations were then waived without the student's failing the course. The chap from Borculo probably needed the credit. Professor Rooks' temperament was even and his demeanor self-effacing. When he was

Prof. A. J. Rooks.

near sixty, his son Albertus Calvijnus was born. Some students placed a large doll in a baby buggy, assembled a brass band, and led a large group past his home in triumphant acclaim. Later that morning the dean served the entire student body ice-cream bars in the college basement after which all went to the chapel where the dean made a speech, quoting St. Paul to the effect that whatever a man sets out to do let him do with all his might. When his retirement at seventy became imminent, Roger Heyns wrote an editorial in the *Chimes* beseeching the Board to permit him to continue for a few more years. This was done under a special arrangement. Even after he was very near the final snowline, he would still walk slowly and absent-mindedly about the campus.

Professor Schoolland, whom Rooks calls his "yokefellow," was very influential during the early years of the college both through his teaching and writing. All accounts stress his distinguished appearance and meticulous attention to the "fine points" of linguistic studies.

Professor Vanden Bosch says, "The study of fine points in etymology
and in grammatical forms and constructions was his joy." Vanden
Bosch admits that such erudite interests suited the graduate student
better than the college student. A very able former student says,
"The first day we read 70 lines; the second day we reviewed and
got to line 45 or so; it must have been two or three weeks before
we got to line 71." That may be an exaggeration, but one does get
the impression that obviously keen scholarship was sometimes un-
wisely applied. Dr. Henry Ryskamp calls him a "thorough teacher,"
easily sidetracked, however, by his philological passion. He was an
exacting teacher as well; once he expressed his disappointment with
improper preparation by saying, "You spoil me my breakfast."
Vanden Bosch also comments on his love of the classics, even though
this love sometimes disturbed him. He also stresses the fact that students felt that they had been "in the stimulating presence of an able
scholar and had undergone the impact of a great mind." His love
of the "fine points" apparently extended to the grading system, since
I have been reliably informed that he gave one student a final grade
of 99¾.

Schoolland wrote many trenchant articles in *De Wachter, De
Calvinist,* and magazines even less known today. He wrote on many
subjects: politics, ethics, psychology, pedagogy. In all these writings
he insisted that Calvinistic principles were essential to American life
and that an institution of higher learning dedicated to their explica-
tion and development was necessary. Such an institution should confront the apostate philosophies of secular higher education with a
comprehensive system of thought based on the Bible, which he
studied with great diligence and in an independent way, and the Reformed faith. Professor Zwaanstra says in his *Reformed Thought and
Experience in a New World* that Schoolland believed that "the
success of the school would be entirely dependent upon the ability
scientifically to form men in whom Calvinistic principles were paramount." These Christian principles rested ultimately upon "an immediate intuition of faith." This intuition, which views the entire
creation in the light of its Creator and His word, is the presuppo-
sition of all knowledge, to which reason must be supportive. Schoolland made frequent use of the word *antithesis,* and Zwaanstra says
that to Schoolland "the antithesis was absolute." He wrote ninety
articles on the subject in *De Calvinist,* in which he maintained that
one was either of the Kingdom of God or of the Kingdom of Satan;
there was no neutrality. He wanted separate political and social or-

ganizations and downgraded common grace. Yet when he once commented to a group of colleagues that "the world would be better off if all books were burned except the Bible"—he paused a few moments and added—"and Plato." As Emerson says, "He builded better than he knew." His was a resonant voice in the early years of the college. He was, as Vanden Bosch says, "a European teacher in an American college," but his rigorous standards, love of Calvinistic ideals, emphasis on the antithesis, and vital transmission of Dutch Calvinism made him a man of commanding importance to the college in his time.

Another influential teacher of these early years was Professor Rinck, whose death in an automobile accident November 11, 1920, was, as Rooks says, "the saddest and most tragic incident in the history of our institution." He was by all accounts a brilliant teacher. Dr. Ryskamp says that he was "a very firm, a very precise individual, impatient with students whose work was sloppy or inaccurate." Something of a martinet, his rigorous methods produced results. Legend has it that he once set the clock back to prolong the period. He also served the college well as secretary and registrar. His death was keenly felt in the small college of that day.

He was the first of five of Calvin's faculty who died in their youth or at the peak of their powers: Tony Brouwer, Harmon Hook, Leonard Vander Lugt, and Henry Zylstra. All their gifts, so important to the college, were stilled at an early age. In 1920 as on the later occasions, the fragility of life and the wise but inexplicable Providence of God were solemnly impressed on the faculty.

The sturdily growing college faced a series of problems which precipitated searching, even searing, debate and required formidable intellectual, moral, and spiritual energy. The main questions were these: What shall the purpose of the college be? What will the nature of the curriculum be? Who shall be the teachers? Who shall control the institution? A sizable pamphlet could be written on any of these matters. The ideal of the college received a good deal of attention, and one of the most interesting explicators of this ideal was Professor B. K. Kuiper.

Kuiper's little book *The Proposed Calvinistic College at Grand Rapids,* 1903, has a quaint, abiding charm and intellectual interest with its Dutchisms, poetic color, historical perspectives, critical idealism, and intemperate attacks upon Hope College. After a terse but moving narrative on the courage, faith, and endurance of the early settlers, Kuiper moves boldly to a blunt challenge: The Dutch should become Americans. God has blessed us, says Kuiper, and the first necessity of material security has been met; now it is time to provide the more important necessities of the spirit. With ominous signs of decay about us, with apostasy and addiction to luxury threatening us, it is time to recommit ourselves to the Kingdom and to sacrifice for its sake. It is our spiritual task to apply the principles of Calvinism to the educational process from the first grade through the seminary. We need to enter American life and influence, but we need a thorough educational system to do that. We need a college as an "intellectual center," and that college must be "first and last an institution of learning," a place not only where parents can "safely send their children," but one in which Calvinism will radiate light on all subjects. Such a college must transcend "a *denominational* college in the narrow sense of the word." We owe this college "to our church and to our country; above all we owe it to God." To that end the members of the Christian Reformed Church must give until they "have suffered on account of it."

It took courage to write this book in 1903. The people were not ready for it; prominent clergy opposed the idea that the college should first of all be a place of learning. The community was not ready to sacrifice for it, and the idea of transcending parochial limits was not welcomed with a shout. It is all the more unfortunate, therefore, that the book is marred by gratuitous and unsupported attacks upon Hope College.

B. K. Kuiper was an eccentric, paradoxical, and enigmatic man. Outspoken and heroic in opinion, he urged intelligent Americanization with no deliberate speed; he wanted the English language to prevail without imperilling the Reformed heritage. He was appointed a professor in the Literary Department of the Theological School in 1900. There he taught, at times brilliantly, until 1918, when he resigned, complaining in *De Wachter* of intolerable pay. Obviously, as the records show and his writings attest, he was a man of imagination, scholarship, droll wit, and rigorous convictions. He was also prone, as the records show, to serene indolence, intemperate enthusiasm, and erratic behavior. According to his students, his preparation was fitful. He apparently hoped when unprepared to receive a few good questions; when he did he rose to the occasion with dramatic success and zest. Some students were permanently impressed by these imaginative flights; others took advantage of the outbursts and even wandered about the room. Kuiper was sometimes tardy as well as unprepared, apparently exhausted by weekend visits to his sweetheart. His absentmindedness was exploited. The teachers' desks in the old Franklin building were placed on little platforms eight inches from the floor. Once the students had moved Kuiper's desk to the very edge of the platform, and as he leaned heavily on it, he and the desk went on to the main floor. The best students waited for the vision; some enjoyed the interruption of duty. Professor Kuiper had a gift for mismanaging his talents as well as for using them.

After his resignation, he accepted work as Editorial Manager in the Eerdmans-Sevensma Publishing House. Synod urged him to return to his duties, but he refused. The same Synod of 1918 appointed him Editor of *De Wachter,* where he, as Dr. Beets of *The Banner,* loyally championed the cause of Calvin College. In a vitriolic exchange in 1922 with H. J. Kuiper, who had questioned the importance Calvin placed on academic excellence, B. K. Kuiper maintained the crucially important value of scholarship; without it the college would be inferior, however Reformed. He says, "If one is oh so very Reformed, but not scholarly, then as a *professor* he is worth exactly *nothing.*" He resigned from Eerdmans in 1923, and in 1926 he was unexpectedly appointed to the chair of Historical Theology at Calvin Seminary. While at the seminary, where he proved to be a powerful teacher, he went to a movie—to several movies. Somebody saw him go. The Curatorium investigated and Kuiper explained that he had gone now and then "to understand the American people." He had quit, he added, when a minister told him he was a stumbling block to the young people. The Curatorium rejected his reappointment. Kuiper was exceptionally unfortunate that the stringent rules against worldly amusements were under consideration at this Synod. He had not danced; he had not played cards; no, but he had seen a movie! He insisted upon a public defense. My father, who was a member of that Synod, told me that Kuiper had talked interminably—more than three hours in fact. His talents were apparent as was his lack of good sense. If he had only said, "I'm sorry. I won't do it again," my father remarked, he would have been reappointed. But that was not his nature and he lost his position. I don't think the movies or even the idea of being free to go to the movies was worth the loss of his services.

The remainder of this talented man's life was mournful. His sources of income were spotty and uncertain; the patience and pocketbooks of his friends became exhausted. He, with much prodding, produced one good book, a biography of Luther. With all his talents he ended as a withered branch. While I was studying at North-

western University, I often left for Chicago or came home from
there around midnight. I saw him frequently between eleven and
twelve walking the almost deserted streets, or just standing on a
corner chewing a dead cigar. It must have been 3 a.m. in his soul.
I was reminded of the sad words of Edwin Arlington Robinson:

> *Familiar as an old mistake*
> *And futile as regret.*

Relations between the church and American society, which
Kuiper discussed, were often tense and disagreeable. The idea of as-
similating such a society or transforming its indifference, even contempt, was not universally appealing. Anyone who grew up in our
church in the early decades of the century and attended either the
Christian or the public schools or both as I did knows there was then
not the easy, or even admired, acceptance of our institutions in the
world about us that there is today. They were often suspect, the
objects of disdain and mindless criticism. As a boy I was often more
inclined to clobber the Scotch-Irish youth in Grundy Center, Iowa,
than to identify with them, let alone change them. Most of us heard
some version of the song:

> *Dutchman, Dutchman,*
> *Bellyful of straw,*
> *Can't say nothin'*
> *But yah, yah, yah.*

Many in the church dreaded the American scene, saw it full of
danger; they felt that Americanization meant loss of distinctiveness.
Some went so far as to consider use of the Dutch language essential
to purity of doctrine. In this atmosphere Kuiper's words were not
always welcome. But Kuiper saw nothing racial or ethnic in Calvinism; neither the Dutch language nor ecclesiastical taboos had anything to do with it. He and later Dr. Clarence Bouma eloquently
pleaded for involvement and impact upon that world whatever the
hazards or resistance. Kuiper argued for the speedy death of Dutch
in the church service either by neglect or asphyxiation. No one who
has not lived through these years knows how bitter the struggle over
the use of the English language was. My father had an elder in the
church at Wellsburg who refused to serve in the consistory for an
entire year because church services were in German instead of Dutch!
Identifying the use of Dutch with religious sanctity was something
Kuiper opposed. These tensions embarrassed and angered some of the

young so that the magnificent tradition embodied in the language was sometimes slighted. It is to the great credit of *Chimes,* the Calvin College paper founded in 1907, that it was peacefully bilingual until the early twenties.

Professor Kuiper and others had defined and championed an ideal for the college which it has attempted to achieve. In essence it is described in the catalog of 1973-74. It aims to give an "education that is Christian and is governed by the Christian faith as reflected in the Reformed standards." It seeks to make this education available not only to members of the Christian Reformed Church, not only to evangelical Protestants, but to others genuinely interested in it.

What kind of curriculum will insure the realization of such an ideal? The faculty of the early years of the century did not wrestle with this problem. As Dr. William Harry Jellema in his highly stimulating pamphlet "The Curriculum in a Liberal Arts College," 1958, observes:

> Beginning some thirty-four years ago, the older generation gradually built our original school into a four year college, granting an A.B. degree. But for an academic blueprint they simply went to the State University.

This curriculum in itself was not ideally suited to the needs of the college. The pre-seminary course, however, did prepare the student well for the seminary, and its sequence of courses went a long way toward assuring a liberal education. In 1963 strenuous efforts were made to revise the curriculum. Calvin College has over the years been much concerned with additions to and modifications of the curriculum; but it never really dealt with the problem as to whether the curriculum itself was valuable in sharpening and applying Christian perspectives on learning. It assumed that the transmission of these principles was pedagogically insured whatever the pattern of subjects. The attempt to construct a new curriculum will be described in a separate chapter. There is no space in this little book to analyze or describe the perennial additions to the curriculum. A detailed account of these matters would preempt the book and the reader. While a curriculum is a very important matter, I should never equate its importance with that of the faculty. A good faculty can squeeze a lot out of a poor curriculum, but no curriculum will rescue a mediocre faculty.

A good faculty is never easy to assemble. It is particularly difficult to assemble in a Christian college and even more difficult when that Christian college is dedicated to a specific interpretation of Christianity. The prospective faculty member should not only be highly knowledgeable in his subject; he should be familiar with the philosophical and theological perspectives of the Reformed tradition and be able to integrate them fruitfully with his learning. He should also be able to teach—not a humdrum attainment either. If you find a person qualified in these matters, he is probably gifted enough to obtain a position in an institution paying a higher salary; so he has to be an idealist. He faces a harder task in a college like Calvin than elsewhere because not only must he know his subject but he has to be able to interpret it in the light of his faith—an immensely complex matter. I do not think it immodest to say that over the years Calvin has enjoyed the services of many such teachers. To obtain them, the earlier rather informal processes of appointment were made much more precise and extensive. Even in the fifties, when appointments were numerous, screening and interviewing on various levels was done with great care. Hard effort went into obtaining properly qualified candidates. President Spoelhof has taken much pride in the quality of the faculty and with sound reasons.

Idealism, however, usually has to be supported by money, and during the second decade of the century the college was becoming increasingly costly. Furthermore, some from other places resented paying for the education of students from Grand Rapids. How was the money to be raised? There were those who held to the view of Abraham Kuyper that a church has no right to control and support a college. This is the business of a society of interested Christians. Others, pietistically bent and influenced by American pragmatism, felt that the church had a duty to all its children, and that even if the principle of societal control were ideally correct, ecclesiastical control was not wrong. Those who have held this view have always thought that the college had no future economically or spiritually without ecclesiastical support and control. Attempts to form a Society for Higher Education proved dismally ineffective. The fact was, as Stob asserts, "The Christian Reformed *community* could not be interested in setting up a college." The Synod of 1908, therefore, accepted a resolution of the Advisory Committee of Synod, which although under periodic attack has been the church's policy ever since. It is worth quoting exactly:

> Your committee recommends that the college remain connected with the Church in this sense that the Church shall support and

maintain her and shall exercise the highest authority over her:

1. Because the Church will then have greater assurances that in the College the special needs which in our land must be met for those who prepare for the ministry will be observed.

2. Because it seems that the College financially will have greater security when she will remain connected with the Church rather than severed from it.

3. Because it is not very well possible for practical considerations that a College be in another way supported and controlled.

The advocates of societal control of the college have never devised a practical plan to replace this resolution, and although over the years tuition has furnished an increasingly large amount of the cost of the college, the income derived from the quota system has been huge. In 1968, President Spoelhof stated in an interview reported in *Chimes* that even then the Christian Reformed Church was contributing $843,000 a year. This sum is equal to the derivable income of an endowment fund of millions and amounts to a subsidy of $240 per student. When John Calvin Junior College was approved in 1906, Synod raised the quota per family per year from fifty-five cents to sixty cents. Today the churches in the Grand Rapids and nearby areas pay a quota of forty-four dollars per family per year. The drastic and certain loss of revenue resulting from a change to societal control has proved unacceptable. Stob says, "The Church is afraid to let the College go." That may be so, but what she fears may not so much be losing control of the college but seeing it die. The cost of hitching a wagon to a star sometimes means losing the wagon.

Although Synod has exercised final authority over the college, the Curatorium has served as its responsible agent in governing the college and in fact has exercised a good deal of authority at all times. The Board of Trustees, elected by Synod, has served the college assiduously and nobly over many years not only in its control of the college but in recommending it for support and student attendance. It has often done so in the face of hostile criticism. Members of the Board have visited the classrooms regularly to report on teachers without permanent tenure. I understand that today the judgments based on such visits are made available to faculty members. Beginning in the fifties the members of the Board have been invited to meet in conference with the faculty in the fall; and in the last years the faculty has been invited to meet with the Board in the February session. The Board meets regularly twice a year, and the meetings are packed with hard work, from evaluating teachers to assessing financial reports. The Board of Trustees has been indispensable in Calvin's history and the college owes it a formidable debt.

What was the spirit of the student body during the early years; years of growth, maturation, Americanization, and yet of a remarkable homogeneity? It is difficult to characterize the spirit of an institution with three distinct student bodies. The youngsters in knickerbockers or the young girls in long dresses were hardly deeply concerned about the "anti-Biblical spirit of the age, tending toward pantheism, agnosticism and materialism." On the other hand, seminarians were being specifically trained to serve a church still strongly rooted in the spirit of the Afscheiding. The college students, whose spirit is best discovered by reading the *Chimes*, were decidedly concerned about the spiritual welfare of the college. The essays in which the early volumes of *Chimes* abound are serious, well-developed, and markedly spiritual in tone and critical judgment. Calvin even then faced problems maintaining enthusiasm for its heritage. Following the lead of Dr. Van Lonkhuyzen, who criticized a "spirit [of indifference] among the students," *Chimes* of February 1918 contains an editorial entitled "Alarm." The editorialist concedes that it is not a false alarm, since "It cannot be denied that there is a certain amount or even a great deal of indifference to Calvinism." This the writer deplores as "a serious thing for Calvin College." In attempting to explain such apathy, the writer suggests the following reasons: indifference, a mistaken conception of Calvinism as dead orthodoxy, too much bloated advertising of its virtues, and weariness with a "man incessantly talking Calvinism." Whatever the cause, the writer urges intelligent enthusiasm for what he regards as a precious heritage.

The defense did not rest. In a later *Chimes*, Nicholas J. Monsma writes a letter to the editor. He admits that some may "over-advertise" Calvinism but argues that a true enthusiast can hardly keep silent. Monsma bristles at what was to become frequent—the humorous use of the word "Calvinism": "It seems to be the pet method of some to ridicule Calvinism." This, incidentally, has been a pet method in and out of our circles by people vaguely disliking the system and lacking or refusing to use the brains essential to master it. Since the word cannot be shelved, and the system itself was never parochial, it would seem that the word should be used and the system understood and applied. Another sturdy defender was R. B. Kuiper. He saw a rather dark future for Calvinism because of worldly-mindedness and Phariseeism in our church. The Phariseeism alienates the young because they tend to identify Calvinism with attending church three times a Sunday, hallowing the Dutch language, and sitting on the porch all Sunday when not in church. He also notes the insidious threats of Methodism with its emphasis on emotionalism, and of traditionalism without insight or passion. In addition, there is the deplorable fact of division in the church between those partially Americanized and the more recent immigrants who wished to retain the old ways. We all have to "know Calvinism" and "know America," said Kuiper, and one important way to achieve this is through sermons "in which relentlessly hard lines are drawn."

The tensions analyzed in these pieces were mild and they are mildly reported. They illustrate in a gentle way the clash of tradition with a growing critical temper which a college never lacks. In the sixties the clash and the tone became stentorian. However painful such tensions are, they are an inescapable concomitant of a college both Christian and scholarly. One mark of the quality of the administration and faculty is the way in which such tension is handled.

The college was now approaching a four-year curriculum. In 1915 and again in 1916, the faculty had asked the Board to add a fourth year. In 1916 there were sixty-seven students in the college; in 1917-18, there were sixty-four. In 1918 the enrollment rose to eighty. For some years increasingly frequent recommendations urged the appointment of a president. Synod decided to appoint an Educational Secretary, whose main duty was to raise money; it felt that a president might have "too much influence on the course of events." But the Synod of 1918 agreed to a recommendation from the Board that a president was needed to "work out an educational policy, to simplify the administration of the school, and to represent the school to the outside world." After Professor Louis Berkhof had declined the appointment, the Reverend Mr. John J. Hiemenga accepted it and assumed the presidency in September 1919.

World War I affected the college in several hard ways. The enrollment dropped and some of the students called up for service were wounded, though none lost their lives. Some elements in Grand Rapids regarded the college, particularly some of the professors, as pro-German. *The Tradesman,* a jingoistic weekly, accused the Calvin professors of treason and suggested that the guilty be lined up against the wall and shot. Dr. Beets defended the college and staff. He granted that some of the professors were anti-British since they remembered the Boer war, but that fact did not make them pro-German. In retrospect the spirit of the time is hard to believe. A secret agent went to McBain to check the loyalty of a small group of Germans living there. In Peoria, Iowa, patriots burned a Christian school. I saw an old German physician forced to march until exhaustion at the head of a parade in Grundy Center, Iowa. The war brought first a cold wind on the campus; its aftermath in the twenties, a torrid eruption of fizz and shock.

Calvin College offered its first regular college program in the school year 1920-21. The foundations were sound and have endured. It had an excellent faculty, admirable student body, solid ecclesiastical support, a dynamic president, a devoted Board, viable solutions to perennial problems, and an exalted ideal. It was a venture of faith in a pragmatic and secularizing world. It hoped to embody simultaneously light and salt. It has not always been easy to harmonize the salt and the light, the "mind of conservatism" and "the mind of impact," the militant edge of the antithesis and the vision of "involvement." But the Lord's favor has rested upon the efforts of Calvin College, the tensions have enriched as well as divided the college and the community it has served.

In the ensuing decades, Calvin achieved, as we shall see, "an enviable academic reputation," to use a well-worn slogan. This reputation was attained partly because of the innate caliber of the students who later distinguished themselves at graduate schools, partly because of a faculty that had done so before their arrival, but also because of a rigorous indoctrination into an intellectually tough tradition, which, whatever one may think of its validity, forces its adherents to think. What is even more important is that Calvin at its best has worked hard to integrate faith and learning—no lip service to learning and much ado about faith, no worship of learning and polite gestures to faith.

The church that supported Calvin in 1920 numbered only 18,861 families. The majority were ordinary people, many without a grammar school education, who worked at humble jobs in factories, fields, and shops. Many had no Calvinistic vision of education and saw very little use in a Calvinistic college, or any college for that matter. They believed in "our school," the seminary, but paying for the education of other people's children for other professions irritated them. Some saw value in a Calvinistic college, but resented control by the church. Few today can remember the dread sense of inferiority that undermined vigorous action. Mobilizing substantial support for the college was tough and discouraging, and one remembers the vision, courage, and unshakeable stamina it then required with gratitude. They built a good college; they fostered a good tradition; they served the Kingdom.

CHAPTER THREE

CALVINISTS IN VANITY FAIR

Vanity Fair, as Bunyan has said, "is no new erected business, but a thing of ancient standing." In it the kingdoms of this world set up their most dazzling displays; in it rages a holy war for the soul of man. Calvin became a full-fledged college when the jazz age, which F. Scott Fitzgerald dates as beginning May Day 1919, blazed across the land in all its tinsel, splendor, and sadness. "America was going on the greatest, gaudiest spree in history," says Fitzgerald, "and there was going to be plenty to talk about." All the old revolts and the new outlets found expression in thought, art, and action. Revolt was the order of the day whether one looked at the antics of the young (Let yourself go, baby), or the attacks on the orthodox account of creation or the Christian idea of marriage, or the notion of living one's life as one wished to. Residual Puritanism was shouted down by H. L. Mencken, who characterized fundamentalist preachers as "geysers of pishposh." Orthodox Christianity was considered a stumbling block to beauty, and a hoary barrier to individuality. The big outlets for the newly asserted freedom were bootleg liquor, jazz, sex, and automobiles, which by increasing mobility increased opportunity. College boys in their raccoon-skin coats staggered in the aisles of the Lackawanna Railroad, passing hip-flasks about on their way to Cornell. Victorian morality, invented by fussy old maids, was to be shattered; old ideas were to be junked with the aid of Marx, Darwin, and Freud. World War I in its aftermath was introducing the "aspirin age," and many were to need it.

America was on the move and big changes rolled over the land. The Anglo-Saxon domination of politics was eroding; farms were emptying and cities were filling. Mass production replaced the independent craftsman. America unlimited was an implicit slogan, though many sensitive spirits shuddered at the rampant materialism. Fitzgerald himself realized that the country was filled with wrong dreams. He saw something greatly wrong with a society in which young ladies say, "Mom, this is a young man I like and he's floating in money." For years our church had said, "In our isolation lies our strength," but isolation was no longer possible; World War I had sapped its strength. Strong measures were adopted during the twenties to keep the world out; but it became increasingly difficult, and Calvin College became a center of the struggle with the world; the tensions in the church gravitated toward expression there.

The students who attended Calvin in the twenties, whether from Grand Rapids and neighboring areas or from more distant places on one of the fifteen daily passenger trains that steamed into the smoke-filled old Union Station, were by and large on the fringes of the big changes. Not many of their parents shared in the lush economy of the time. None of them participated in the free-wheeling morality of the big cities. Coming from the shelter of pious homes, sound Reformed preaching, and thorough catechetical instruction, they at first heard the new spirit only as a distant drum. But as the drum beat grew nearer over the decade and their studies in college had to take account of it, they found little retreat from personal confrontation. The alien voices in the arts and literature, philosophy and science were both strident and unavoidable. The faculty tried to confront the new culture with understanding, appreciation when deserved, and Reformed assessment.

This attempt on the part of the faculty, as well as the attitudes of the students toward the new voices, was soon under fire. Already in 1919, J. H. Bruinooge had attempted in the *Chimes* to rebut the charge that by showing a genuine interest in art, philosophy, and science Calvin was drifting into modernism. His defense was Kuyperian—the students should not concern themselves only "with the future life." They should uphold "the honor of our King in every sphere of life." Such sincere statements have never satisfied a certain element in the church. In 1921 *The Witness* appeared *against* the profession of such an attitude. The Reverend Mr. H. J. Kuiper launched an attack upon Calvin, "out of love," hoping that people "will not take it ill when we begin to criticize our Seminary and Calvin College." He was greatly disturbed when he heard the Glee Club sing "The Rosary," and that W. Smith, a Mason, had addressed the students on Armistice Day. He would write a series of articles faulting the administration and the intellectual, spiritual, and social life of the college. He wrote a harsh article against President Hiemenga, whom he in effect accuses of having sold out to scholarly excellence at the price of Reformed integrity. B. K. Kuiper responded with a red-hot editorial in *De Wachter* and a vitriolic debate between the two ensued. B. K. Kuiper maintained that the charges were false and that Calvin could be and was both scholarly and Reformed. The debate simmered down because H. J. Kuiper could not furnish convincing proofs. Calvin College, however, has had to live its entire life under this kind of concern and in doing so has had many anxious moments.

The concern about Calvin was not restricted to the lofty areas of art, philosophy, and theology. There were many concrete, every-day matters that worried parents: the radio with its jazz and slang, the movies, and bobbed hair. Professor Swets remarks in his fine book *Fifty Years of Music at Calvin College* that a good Sioux County grandma, speaking in the Dutch language, asked the visiting singers, "Now boys, how is it all at Calvin College? Is there any religion left or is it all English?" Some of the students were decidedly Puritan in outlook. One of them goes so far as to deplore a mock-election. He felt strongly that in doing so we were "imitating the world," since such an election had been held in a public high school. He exhorts, "We must banish everything that smacks of worldliness." Worldliness as exhibited in the three forms condemned by Synod in 1928—movie attendance, card playing, and dancing—was a ticklish, even explosive, problem at Calvin for the next quarter century.

In response to these pressures, the faculty exercised a decidedly paternalistic role in the twenties, not so much through individual and personal interviews, which though mandatory were often neglected, but rather through rules about morals and manners. Most important were the regulations against worldliness as expressed in card-playing, dancing, and movie attendance. Abraham Kuyper, in his Stone Lectures delivered at Princeton in 1898, had condemned them as "The *Rubicon* which no Calvinist could cross without sacrificing his earnestness to dangerous mirth." But moral persuasion by faculty and president did not stop movie attendance. By 1926 the Board took strong action. It decided not only to warn students about these activities but to expel them if they were confirmed in them and refused to desist. The rules never achieved much; they were simply impossible to enforce with any consistency or fairness. The college also published a quaint little period piece, *College Conduct*. Conceived in genuine concern, it reflects not only that spirit of concern but also the mood of the social authorities of the time. One of the marks of loyalty is, it says, "a willingness to sacrifice past habits in the interest of the college," a notion of loyalty hardly acceptable by students of our time. What do well-mannered students do? The well-bred college girl "completes her toilette in her room," and is "scrupulous about avoiding any conduct at night that might possibly give rise to comment by any observer." The college man "never properly takes an arm or offers his arm to the girl on the street, unless it is really necessary for him to assist her in crossing a muddy or slippery place." Furthermore, the girl "merely rests the palm of her hand lightly within the curve of his elbow." No "well-bred student ever wears conspicuous clothing." When he eats he "sits up straight . . . spreads his napkin half-open across his lap . . . and puts a small amount of food on his fork at a time." Eat pickles with your fingers and slice off a whole slice of bread and chew off portions. I may add that I remember well the fun we had with this little book in the twenties: it was a crushing example of lack of communication even then. It must have been an embarrassment to many on the staff, just as the absolutism about movie attendance was answered by no real involvement in the problem on the part of the faculty. Many young men, many young women, even some pre-sems, went to an occasional movie. The problem, however, was to become more acute in the thirties; and no one who has not lived through these times can realize what a headache it was, because everybody knew there were good pictures to see and, what we now know, none as perverse as some of those freely attended by students today.

Most of the students had little money, but they did not need a great deal in 1920. Tuition was thirty dollars a year with a reduction if you came from a distant place. "Bed, room, fuel and light in good families" was seven dollars a week; board and room in the dormitory, ready for occupancy in the fall of 1924, was six dollars a week for a double room. Clothes were relatively inexpensive. At J. R. Trompen, where men's apparel was "not foppish but that crowning excellence of pep and smartness," suits or a fur-lined overcoat could be had for twenty-five dollars. H. Bragt did shaves and haircuts for a quarter. Gunn Sectional Bookcases were only $29.50 and desks for home use only $13.50. Coffee and toasted cheese sandwiches (better known today as grilled cheese) could be had for fifteen cents. Motion pictures, which were forbidden, were twenty-five to fifty cents, with a Saturday matinee setting one back ten cents. The streetcar you shouldn't take to get there cost a nickel. Letters home reminding the folk of your good health and need of money cost only two cents to send.

In 1920, Calvin had some 200 students and twenty professors. It had in 1919 acquired the Reverend Mr. J. J. Hiemenga as its first president. But he presided over a faculty accustomed to years of democratic control under the mild leadership of Dean Rooks. He inherited no tradition, few clearly defined duties, no faculty handbook with valuable guidelines for policy. The faculty had largely run the school, referring only matters of crucial importance to the Board. Though there was good will on the faculty, they were not accustomed to looking for leadership outside their own ranks. Yet a president must assume leadership; he must have "influence on the course of events," particularly in an American college. American college presidents have always been expected to lead, to provide vision, idealism, and at least a certain amount of managerial talent. Presidents are important in American colleges; they set the tone of the institution and are the persons most likely to face the challenges of the day. Each president of Calvin has put his stamp on the institution and this should be fairly recorded. President Hiemenga had no precedent to follow, but he did have, as we shall see, his own well-defined and meaningful vision. He came to a school in excellent academic order. In some ways his presidency would have to blaze a new trail, and much depended upon his personality. He knew the problem. He summed it up in an interview with Dr. Herbert Brinks: "At the very beginning, I was up against it because I was the first president."

President Hiemenga was an eloquent preacher, a forceful leader, and a very hard worker. He had attended Columbia University while serving a congregation in Passaic, New Jersey, and had earned an M.A. degree. He was accustomed to high congregational esteem. A man of many talents, gracious concern, and deep commitment to the future of Calvin, he did not, however, fully overcome the resistance of the faculty. President Hiemenga did not feel fully at home at the college. "When I was President of Calvin College," he says, "I missed my congregation." He resigned in 1925, but not until he had accomplished a great deal.

President Hiemenga had proposed a significant program for the college in the spring of 1920. This program exhibits imagination, idealism, and courage. In the first place he urged the immediate beginning of a high school so that Calvin could serve only one student body—the college students. He urged strongly that the Christian school cooperate closely under Calvin's leadership. Calvin itself should be so developed that it is "able to compete with any institution of its kind." To the three courses offered must be added a normal course. The staff must be increased. He spelled out its immediate needs: a boys' dormitory, a gymnasium, a million-dollar endowment

President J. J. Hiemenga.

fund. None of these goals was easy, and it is surprising to note how much he accomplished in his brief presidency.

H. J. Kuiper's attacks upon the goal of scholarly excellence, as if sound learning imperilled piety, found ready ears, as such attacks always have in Calvin's history, and impeded the attainment of an endowment fund, although through the president's efforts and those of the Reverend Mr. J. Vander Mey almost $100,000 was raised. The project was dropped. The *Chimes* of November 1924 says of President Hiemenga:

> In spite of many difficulties he engineered a campaign which resulted not only in our Dormitory, but which made possible a suitable place for our athletic activities.

Former President Hiemenga's account of his acquisition of $40,000 of this money for the dormitory from Mr. William Van Agthoven of Cincinnati is fascinating. When he informed the Board that he wished to make a trip to Cincinnati to ask Van Agthoven for a gift, they said, "You don't have to go there. He'll give you ten dollars and it'll cost you more than ten dollars to go there and come back again." Hiemenga arranged to preach there; he paid his own fare. Van Agthoven met him with horse and buggy and took him for a ride about Cincinnati. He gave him $10,000 and promised another $10,000 if Hiemenga would raise a similar amount elsewhere. Hiemenga went back to Grand Rapids with ten negotiable $1,000 bonds in a brief case. He went back three times and garnered $40,000 in all—a goodly sum for the times. He raised $80,000 for the Dormitory, valued at $140,000 and containing a gymnasium where the equipment, in the words of Dean Rooks, "comprises all the apparatus necessary to the latest and most approved physical exercise." It was occupied in the fall of 1924.

Hiemenga did not favor introducing a normal course at Calvin. He said years later, "I never meant, you know, that a Normal School should be a part of Calvin College, it shouldn't be." He had wanted the National Union of Christian Schools to undertake this work. Since they were unable to do so and since the Superintendent of Public Schools in Michigan required all teachers in Michigan to have a diploma in three years, he felt Calvin had to help. If Calvin were to add a few professors and courses, it could avert a crisis. The college recommended the appointment of Henry Van Zyl, whom they subsidized for a year at the University of Chicago. Though neither Hiemenga nor Johannes Broene, his successor, favored the training of teachers at Calvin, such preparation has become an important part of Calvin's program.

When President Hiemenga left the college in 1925 to accept the pastorate of the Christian Reformed church in Lafayette, Indiana, the faculty advised the Board to appoint an acting president for one year. This would allow more time for a considered appointment. They recommended Johannes Broene and Jacob G. Vanden Bosch, neither of whom was attracted to the position. When the Board appointed Johannes Broene, Vanden Bosch graciously wrote, "All lovers of Calvin rejoice in this selection." He praises Broene's scholarship, pedagogical skill, and character and concludes by saying, "He richly deserves the distinction conferred upon him." In the same issue of the *Alumni Letter,* Professor Broene praises Vanden Bosch for twenty-five years of distinguished services to the college. The early members of the Calvin faculty had a penchant and a gift for this sort of exchange. The faculty welcomed the appointment, not only because they respected Broene highly, but also because he would not diminish their participation in the councils of the college. It would be a quiet administration without programmatic bustle or disturbing innovation.

The presidency of J. Broene was academically oriented; the emphasis in the college was upon effective teaching and scholarship devoted to that end. Grants for independent research were unknown and never asked for. Faculty writing, what there was of it, was largely restricted to religious publications serving the Christian Reformed Church, or to semi-popular journals serving elements in the same group. Most of the social activities of the students were academically directed: clubs, forensics, student publications. Athletics was just beginning to be noticed. Musical organizations were sparse; there were no dramatic productions. One of the reasons that movie attendance became so fiery an issue lies in the limited opportunities for many students in the way of amusements. Since Calvin's amusements were so largely intellectual, many students looked to "worldly amusements" for diversion and solace.

The small faculty, which never numbered more than seventeen during the twenties, not only established the distinctive character of the college and its early good reputation, but also exerted an enormous influence upon its future development. It was a young faculty, and its influence lasted many years. Professor William Harry Jellema and Professor Henry Ryskamp, for instance, were at Calvin until the early sixties. The faculty was small, able, and idiosyncratic enough to be well known to the entire student body either through the classroom or chapel. Students learned to know professors in their major subjects very well. The members of this faculty exercised an enormous influence upon future faculty members by their teaching and by their role in determining new appointments. This faculty cast a long shadow in Calvin's history.

The faculty of the twenties was strikingly varied in academic training, personality, and teaching methods. In 1929 there were only two Ph.D.'s on the staff, although three more had attained this academic union card by 1932. The lecture method was heavily employed; a few used a recitation method. Classroom discussion was little sought or used, though Dr. Jellema often employed the Socratic method brilliantly. The faculty regarded the students with unobtrusive friendliness; there was no "Just call me Phil" atmosphere. The student usually solved his own problems, including those of registration. The faculty were willing to counsel upon request, and some did so with time-consuming generosity. But guidance and counselling, the whole elaborate system of shepherding students through college, was not yet a little cloud on the horizon. Professors were assigned to spiritual counselling, but it was not done with uncontrollable enthusiasm or frequency. The major effort of the faculty went into the duties of competent teaching and the attempt to apply Reformed principles to subject matter. Some did this with animation and insight, some with animation, still others with insight, and a few with neither.

Former President Johannes Broene, who held the presidency from 1925-30, and who expressed the tone of the institution rather than set it, wrote in *The Banner* of July 27, 1928, "Here at Calvin numbers interest us very little." He wished no army of students among whom would then be students lacking ability, health, interest, money, and malleability. "College," says Broene flatly, "is not for the masses." Attendance at Calvin, he often asserted, is a privilege not a right. The students whom Calvin welcomes are not only willing to study but "willing too, to abide by such regulations as are deemed necessary." There is, of course, an elitist ring to all this, and re-

College faculty in the twenties.

cruitment was in his day nonexistent. His major concern was the liberal arts program. He disliked giving credit for courses in professional training: he wished to give "mathematics a place of honor in our curriculum but not engineering." Every subject is to be taught from Reformed perspectives in a way that encourages thinking, not regurgitation. Finally, although "the most important thing in a college is its faculty," the faculty "exists, as everything else here exists—for the students."

The faculty at Calvin has always had to operate under a complex set of loyalties not always mutually supportive or harmonious. The Calvin professor has a loyalty to his subject, to scholarly investigation and integrity, but he also has a loyalty to the church that employs him, whose members have widely varied convictions about economics, politics, the nature and interpretation of various other disciplines, and the place and character of amusements in the Christian life. Ethnic ties, personal friendships, and ecclesiastical duties have complicated certain problems even further.

In the twenties and thirties, the faculty was small and closely knit; whatever problems there were involved everyone. Furthermore, the faculty had a great deal of power, and in the thirties, problems and conflicts brought confrontation between the Board and the faculty, in which, since the number of participants were few and all of them were involved, tensions and feelings sometimes ran high. Among the faculty were some very strong personalities whose gifts, interesting and significant in themselves, illustrate the temper of the time, the problems, and some of the attempted solutions.

A powerful influence during these years was Dr. William Harry Jellema, Professor of Philosophy from 1920 to 1935, and later, after serving as Professor of Philosophy at the University of Indiana for a time, from 1948 to 1963. I think it fair to say that Calvin would have been a very different college without his services. A teacher, as one of his distinguished students has said, "without peer in the experience of most of us," he used his manifold talents in the interests of his faith, and, as Nicholas Wolterstorff has said, "at almost every point that faith illuminated his philosophical perception." Henry Stob, a distinguished teacher of philosophy at Calvin and later a professor at Calvin Seminary, said, "Like Plato and Augustine he is concerned to impart to his students a philosophical vision and a critical awareness"; he was deeply convinced "that Calvinists should acquire a Christian perspective on the whole of life." He was always regarded as an extraordinary teacher, whose influence at Calvin was not restricted to gifted philosophy majors, but permeated the temper of the student body and counted heavily in the councils of the college. He achieved this by a strikingly winning personality, profound vision, and imaginative and magnetic teaching, not by a corpus of learned books, a sacrosanct system of thought, or disciples with badges and trumpets.

Many non-philosophy majors like myself were attracted to Dr. Jellema's classes because we experienced there a brave, new world of thought, insight, and commitment which permanently enriched us, though we neither could nor tried to be philosophers. Jellema introduced students to the drama of ideas; he made you feel that the unexamined life was unworthy of a student, that the life of the mind was not only inherently important but immensely interesting, and that the mind with which you confronted experience reached the heart of the matter. When he applied the Socratic method to some self-appointed genius, you not only enjoyed the deflation, but you learned something about thinking. When he lectured on the great philosophers, you got to know them from the inside, you became involved in their thinking; you were not left there, isolated in an alien world, but aided to think your way out to Christian answers. The student was forced to face unsettling problems and sometimes he himself became unsettled. When this happened, unfair rumors eddied about and caused tensions, as we shall see later. When Dr. Jellema returned to Calvin in 1948, he said his main reason for returning was "to develop Calvinistic thought." That had always been his service to Calvin, a service filled with brilliant achievement even in the face of occasional dissent and criticism.

An entirely different but no less staunch advocate of Calvinism was Jacob G. Vanden Bosch, Professor of English for fifty years at Calvin. He was a man of many moods and manners. As J. Broene said of him:

> He has personality, a personality all his own. There is not another Vanden Bosch on the faculty, I do not know whether it would be desirable to have one, but this Vanden Bosch I would not want to lose.

He had his eccentricities, unfortunately more often remembered by his students than his more important talents. The eccentricities were largely genuine, part of the man himself: the relaxed delivery of a lecture from his chair, then the sudden jump into effervescence, pacing about and sometimes whacking a student on the back in his enthusiasm; the memorable reading of a poem and then asking a student who was expected to agree but really might not, "Isn't this poetry, Mr. X?"; the burst of fury after chapel when some speaker had mispronounced *creek* or misinterpreted a text; the petulance with dissent. He knew more students than anyone I have known: he was incurably interested in student romances. He could be very gracious and also chillingly distant. His love for his students, his colleagues, the college, and his Lord were manifest and enduring. He obviously and always, as he stated in *Chimes,* endeavored "to let my Christianity speak in the classroom."

During his long career at Calvin, Professor Vanden Bosch taught an impressive variety of courses in two literatures, in addition to "The Principles of Criticism," "Advanced Rhetoric," and "The Teaching of English." No one could teach so many courses without varying knowledgeability and skill. He was interested in American Literature, especially in the Puritans, of whom he once said, "The way those Puritans have been treated is a monstrosity." In attempting to right the scales, he sometimes overweighted the worth of the Puritans. He was also greatly concerned with the Victorian poets and their alternating anguish of doubt and faith. To this mass of literature he consistently applied an encyclopedic idea of literary criticism rooted in continental Dutch antecedents. He applied ethical principles with great enthusiasm and unfailingly confronted apostasy with Calvinistic convictions. In so doing, he sometimes glutted the students with moralizing, or so they thought, and to compound the assumed offense, did it authoritatively. The task he performed was difficult because he had vocal students who made him aware of their impatience. Among these students was Peter De Vries, whom he once ordered out of class for impertinence; Manfred, a kindly person, but championing markedly different critical perspectives; and especially Dave De Jong, whose resentment still burned years later and flared up into slander in his book *With A Dutch Accent.* Vanden Bosch never compromised in ideals for the sake of peace or popularity, and the vast majority of students respected him for it.

De Jong's attack is an amazingly vitriolic and inaccurate one. He calls Vanden Bosch a "particularly fluffy and lush teacher," neither of which was true. He says, "He made me memorize reams of the more drippy and lachrymose effusions of Longfellow and Tennyson," which is false. I was in some of the same classes with De Jong and we never had to memorize a line of either. He says that in front "of the entire class he called me 'lily-livered, unsavory, un-

couth, and perverse.' " I can't say this was untrue, but in the thirty-
three hours of English I took with Vanden Bosch, I never heard him
use such nasty language in talking to a student even when it might
have been deserved (though he might have used it to describe H. L.
Mencken). He goes on to say that Vanden Bosch taught that
"nothing really great and moral has been produced in American
literature since Helen Hunt Jackson's *Ramona*," published in 1884.
He may have said that, but how much "great and moral literature"
was in fact produced in American Literature between *Ramona* and
1928? If he did say this, he surely would have had the backing of
Paul Elmer More and Stuart P. Sherman. And I know Vanden
Bosch saw great merit in Robinson and Frost. I mention all this to
show the hazards a teacher at Calvin faces; devotion to the ideals
of the school may receive hostile reaction, whether one stimulates
the students to find the answers on his own or gives them authoritatively.

Still another way of stressing Calvinistic principles was that
of infectious enthusiasm for its contributions. This was the way of
Professor Van Andel, Professor of Dutch Language and Literature,
teacher of organ and often chapel organist, voluminous writer for
Calvinistically oriented journals, teacher of Dutch and Medieval
history, Dutch and Flemish Art, and classroom oracle on anything
that diverted his mind from conjugations and declensions. A remarkable man, blessed with many talents, a most imaginative mind, an
ardent spirit, and boundless kindness. His versatility overwhelmed
him, but that he did so many things so well is memorable. There
was a bird-like rapidity of movement in him, in his talk, his gestures, his facial animation. Ideas tumbled from his lips, and he
quivered with enthusiasm whether he showed his picture of the
nude with the apple ("Class, concentrate on the apple") or in later
years drowned you in his enthusiasm for the Philosophy of Law
("Boy, oh Boy!"). He was a brilliantly imaginative teacher of history; the images flashed before you in splendor. He was bored with
Dutch grammar, and fled it whenever he could. Once when he was
criticized because the pre-seminarians did not know enough Dutch,
he said, "Why? I gave them all A's." That he was enthusiastically
committed to Calvinism was obvious, but it sometimes seemed to
his students that he claimed too much for its influence on Dutch
culture, and some of the symbolism he discovered in Dutch paintings
seemed obvious only to him. He shortchanged himself by spreading
himself so thinly, but that was partly due to the exigencies of the

day and his devotion to the school. Admiration for the principles he affirmed so enthusiastically was often stimulated by the caliber of his mind and quality of his spirit.

In the latter twenties, Dr. H. H. Meeter was appointed Professor of Bible. Upon his appointment, Bastian Kruithof, known to many for his exceptional gifts as writer and preacher, wrote in *Chimes* that the "long cherished college chair of Bible was now filled by a man who adds grace and intellect and wisdom to our much honored staff." In addition to teaching inordinately large classes for years, Meeter published in 1939 the book *Calvinism,* of which Professor L. Berkhof said: "We know of no other work in the English language which offers such a concise, and yet complete and thoroughly reliable resumé of the teachings of Calvinism." This book ran into three editions. For years Dr. Meeter taught a course in Calvinism which provided the students with a solid introduction to its basic principles.

These are illustrative accounts of ways in which Calvinistic principles were applied and received in teaching and writing. They do not exhaust the excellent efforts to relate faith and learning in that day. They do, however, exemplify the difficulty of attempting to do so. During all the coming years, as we shall see more explicitly in a later chapter, somebody was ringing the alarm that the Reformed witness of the professors was either inadequate or overblown. Whatever else there was in Zion, there was little ease. What was the prevailing spirit of the students in these times? That is summed up with lofty and windy grandeur in the Epilogue to Benjamin Euwema's poem "Laus Stultitiae":

EPILOGUE

Far from the East they have come, from New Jersey and
  old Massachusetts;
From far-away Kansas' lone prairies, from Fremont, the
  home of good cider;
From Holland and Kalamazoo, from South Holland, Oak
  Park, and Sheboygan;
Come from their homes and their dear ones to live with
  us, be as our brothers.
Cosmic in scope is our body—divided in origin only.
"Aes triplex" and closer than sanguine the bonds which
  do bind us together.
And what in this old world of ours is more dear to the
  soul than real friendship?

> *Let us all join, o my brothers, in singing the praises of*
> *Friendship*
> *As seen to be manifest clearly in "College Inn", Noble*
> *and Peerless!*

Benjamin F. Euwema was a highly gifted student and became a distinguished scholar, teacher, and dean. In this poem he points out a salient feature of student relations to the faculty and to each other—pervasive friendliness.

There was respect, receptivity, and friendliness in the attitude of students to faculty. There was next to no harsh criticism of the faculty, and it never suffered in *Chimes* or *Prism*. Students whined about chapel attendance, but they went. The discipline committee had its problems, but most cases concerned minor matters or what today would be considered no matters at all. There was scant demand for exposure to controversial speakers, little social zeal, in fact little social conscience as we know it today. There were no drums of war, no draft, no bitter racial tensions, no drugs, and few beers. It was a quiet time; the rebels were few. In fact the faculty, compared to the late sixties, had the life of serenity; they enjoyed an estimation and affection rarely expressed today. When Professor A. J. Rooks came back from a trip to Rome, the *Chimes* became ecstatic:

> We are happy . . . . He's got so-many-feet-reserved-choice-frontage-lot location in the hearts of the students, and it's not any blue-sky real estate either; it's solid earth and tender, too. Welcome back Professor.

In 1973 one of Calvin's most distinguished professors retired, and *Chimes* did not honor him with a single line.

How did the students respond to the Calvinistic principles that were taught? If one searches the pages of *Chimes* one finds very little criticism of these principles and a great deal of respectful attention to them. I was especially struck by some devout, even pious, pieces by students who later deserted these principles. If one turns over the pages of memory, one of course encounters the turbulent exceptions, the literary rebels, and others who were openly skeptical but even then respectful. When one reads criticisms of the college, they are largely directed against the ideas of the faculty rather than the ideas of the students. There was in the twenties, I would say, a general and often enthusiastic acceptance of Calvinistic principles, although there were marked exceptions, more fully apparent later. Only in the matter of worldly amusements was there disagreement, disavowal, and disobedience. Few students played cards, not even Rook, few did or even could dance, but despite all rules and admonitions many did go to the movies. Their attendance, especially after the Synodical decisions of 1928, was a vexing and insoluble problem for many years.

The curriculum in the 1920's had been borrowed from the University of Michigan, and although not peculiarly suited to the unique ideals of the college, served those ideals not through its own character but through the ways in which professors used it to apply their own perspectives to its subject matter. The pre-seminary course was rigidly prescribed, heavily linguistic and philosophic in character. The Liberal Arts Courses were divided into three major groups: Languages, Literature, and Public Speaking; the Sciences, which included Logic; and a group which included History, Economics, Sociology, Philosophy, and Education. All liberal arts students were required to take eight hours of Bible, six of Rhetoric, six of Psychology and Logic, six of Philosophy, twelve of German or French, and ten of Science. The remaining sixty-six hours were devoted to majors, in which a good student could acquire a good many courses, and electives. The efforts of the faculty to insure a good education were recognized in an editorial in the *Grand Rapids Press* on March 11, 1926, by the following comment: "Calvin is a builder of character and a trainer of intelligence worth considering as a civic asset as well as a denominational asset in Grand Rapids."

The college student, however, is very rarely wholly in his books and classes. Many significant extracurricular activities were firmly established and solidly developing in these years. The first *Prism* appeared in 1920, calling itself a "book of pleasant recollections" and a "permanent remembrance of the spirit of good fellowship pervading our school." Dr. Henry Beets offered congratulations in *The Banner* and is almost entirely complimentary, finding fault only with "Just Jokes," which he says "should have a little more salt in them." Athletics and music were taking a firm hold on college life, and clubs were proliferating.

No history of Calvin would be either just or complete without serious attention to these clubs, which persisted until the late sixties and fostered significantly the intellectual and spiritual life of the college. The clubs reflected the interests of the students and the spirit of the times. In the earlier years, clubs with such names as Nil Nisi Verum, the Aurora Society, the Lolileen Oratorical Club, the Jowirapabe Historical Club, the Pi Delta Club, De Lesche

CALVIN COLLEGE

*An Institution of the
Christian Ref. Church*

The School that stands for the application of Reformed principles in all its courses. Its aim is thoroughness and completeness. It has a new building with all conveniences and modern equipments. Its courses are given by a large staff of competent teachers. It offers a full Seminary, Classical, Modern Classical and Teacher's course. Tuition only $50.00 per year.

Come to your own school for your education.

Come and enjoy the wholesome spirit of christian fellowship of our school.

For further information correspond with

J. J. HIEMENGA, President,
Calvin College,
Grand Rapids, Mich.

Calvin catalog 1921.

Vereeniging, the K. K. Q.'s, the Knicker Club, and the Philoi Aletheias, among many others, flourished. Later on clubs multiplied until fully half of the student body were participants. Almost every discipline had its club. The Pierian Club studied great writers and stimulated student writers; the Plato Club studied the great thinkers in smoke-filled rooms; the Phytozoon Club enlisted scientists; the Knickerbocker Club devoted itself to history. There were clubs that were short-lived, such as the Neo-Pickwickian Club, which under the humane and genial leadership of Dr. Ryskamp examined writers from Dickens to Tolstoi in odd places from the college attic to a lounge in a downtown hotel. These clubs were not organized, as one hostile critic said, to get their pictures in the *Prism,* though this might not be an unwelcome dividend; they were an expression of intellectual and social needs, and they were remarkably successful in fulfilling them.

Many of these clubs had genuine educational dimensions. Some of them covered at least a semester's work during the course of a year. Carefully prepared papers delivered before their wary and sometimes hypercritical peers generated free-wheeling discussion, often a discipline in precise articulation. These clubs cemented not only friendship but also faith. When they died out, the informal discussions that replaced them were hardly of equal caliber.

The Calvin College *Chimes,* about which more will be said in a later chapter, first appeared in 1907. During its long existence, it has appeared in various formats, published articles in Dutch and English, short stories and verse, struggled with indigence when supported by voluntary subscriptions, luxuriated in means when supported by ample student fees, weathered both praise and condemnation. It has not always articulated the spirit of the student body; sometimes it has raucously trumpeted the personal prejudices of the staff. Its editors and contributors have included many highly gifted students, and in its pages many future writers have hammered out a style.

During the late twenties and early thirties the rather formal magazine included the enigmatic poems of David De Jong, the fiery editorials of Peter De Vries, and poems and short stories by Manfred (Feike Feikema). In the fall of 1930, Peter De Vries inaugurated a journalistic revolution both in form and content. He took on all comers, including the Curatorium, in spicy, hard-hitting prose. Outraged by the failure of this body to introduce student fees he says:

> The 1930 vest pocket edition of the Sanhedrin has vigorously squelched a sincere overture from a groaning student body . . . . [while it] pursues its agenda between huge draughts of Java and stern circumnavigation around the perimeter of doughnuts.

He also introduced the newspaper format, which was abandoned a few years later; not, however, before Dr. Henry Beets, always alert to what went on in the college, had said: "The *Chimes* still appears in magazine style and format, to the regret no doubt of some of the old-timers who prefer the formal makeup of the *Chimes* of other years." Later, in 1947-48, *Chimes* adopted the magazine format permanently. Peter De Vries retired after one semester; I never really knew whether this was due to nervous exhaustion, as he said, or hierarchical duress. De Vries was a wholly unforgettable character, gifted with amazing verbal dexterity expressed also in prize-winning orations and informal conversation; he was academically indolent, and although in many ways an exhibitionist, surprisingly shy about dating. He became a famous novelist, and in all his satirical books, there are, as far as I know, no slurring comments on Calvin College.

Oratory and debate were prestigious activities in these days, and Calvin students were eminently successful in both. The school took great pride in these efforts and often packed the chapel to applaud them.

Professor Seymour Swets' definitive book *Fifty Years of Music at Calvin College* is crammed with interesting details impossible to recount here. Calvin was long interested in music. Already in 1906 an orchestra was given permission to organize; a glee club was organized in 1913, and a varsity quartet in 1922. In that year the "Calvin Friendship Song" was published, written by Raymond Hoekstra with musical accompaniment by Hila Vanden Bosch. In 1923, Professor Swets first conducted Handel's *Messiah,* a function he performed for fifty years. In later years, bands, vocal ensembles, the A Cappella Choir, the radio choir, directed for many years by James De Jonge, and other groups were added. Today the Music Department offers a wide variety of musical education and gives and sponsors many excellent programs.

During all these years Professor Swets, who began his career at Calvin teaching history, music, public speaking, and physics, exercised a profound and dynamic influence on the development of music at Calvin. He brought good music into good standing; he broke down prejudice and provincialism in the church. His genial and open personality enabled him to extend appreciation for good music. He knew the limits to bringing "high-brow" music to the unsophisticated. "Forceful, not ostentatious," as a friend describes him, he did an enormous amount to enhance good feeling for Calvin. It was entirely fitting that the Choral Room in the Fine Arts Center was dedicated to him in 1966.

Athletics, a major student activity and diversion, began shakily in the early years of this era. There was no administrative enthusiasm and little faculty support. The first Athletic Association was formed and approved in 1919, but only intramural basketball was allowed. This did not satisfy the competitive drive of some students, and they organized a self-appointed college team called The Rivals, who played eighteen games against outside teams without faculty approval but with huge success. The record sounds zany. They beat Saranac 2-0 and the All Stars 9-6; yet they annihilated East Grand Rapids High 59-9. The Rivals, who continued to play despite faculty disapproval, were finally disciplined by being denied the right to take final examinations, and the seniors were barred from commencement. Later a varsity team was organized and the kindly William Cornelisse served as coach until disabled by ill health. One of the first intercollegiate games with Hope was followed by such a dramatically destructive aftermath—defacing of property, raucous verbal exchange, and the crunch of fists—that competition was temporarily abandoned.

Athletics at Calvin, even without football, has had an exciting and enviable history. Over the years student participation, both male and female, has been steadily expanded. Calvin has won more than its fair share of MIAA Championships in basketball, and, despite the lack of football, an All Sports Award in the MIAA (Michigan Intercollegiate Athletic Association) in 1969. The justifiable pride Calvin fans take in the teams of Calvin is heightened by the fact that a sane relationship between athletics and the other functions of the college has always been insisted upon by coaches, administration, and faculty. Glory days have been celebrated but with just cause. Athletes have never been recruited in crass and dishonorable ways. Recruiting has been a matter of friendly persuasion rather than cash subsidy. Athletics has always been an extracurricular activity.

As might be expected among good Calvinists, there was also need for a Discipline Committee, which developed through regular exercise. Student pranks had to be dealt with; they have always had to be dealt with from the time in 1915 when Dean Rooks sat on a pin carefully planted in his chair as he was about to lead a chapel service, and Fanny X got two weeks' vacation, to the streakers of 1973. Pranks had been frequent in the erratic housing accommodations in the first years of the century. Housing nonresidents had always been somewhat of a headache; now with the occupation of the new Dormitory in 1925, the headache was at least localized. A good deal of therapeutic horseplay occurred in this place: badly rumpled rooms of supercilious inhabitants; showering a know-it-all with all his clothes on, locking him up in his room, and throwing the wet clothes in the highest branches of the tree beside the dorm, where they froze overnight; arranging a pail of water so that when

President Stob opened the door he received an improper welcome. One student was conned into believing he was a gifted tenor and sang "There's a Wee Hous in the Heather" over a fake radio set-up. Sunday evening meals were dismal affairs of apples, tea, bread, and peanut butter. One seminarian said grace: "Dear Lord, we thank Thee for this light lunch. There may be those who would be happy to share it, but we don't know who they are."

Two rather spectacular pranks occurred in 1930. One evening the Grand Rapids Fire Department came clanging to the dormitory to extinguish what was apparently a dangerously burning roof. After the preliminary furor, a careful examination revealed only a piece of fire-proof material on which a gaudy blaze had been carefully built. In the same year a giant fire-cracker exploded in the Hekman Memorial Library, cracking lights and shaking the volumes. Both events, but especially the latter, greatly disturbed President Broene. After the case had been reviewed by the Discipline Committee, the Student Council and the culprits were called in and the verdict delivered. That was it. No advocates, appeals, channels, or long documents to follow.

One Sunday evening as freshmen Fred Feikema and John De Bie came home from hearing Billy Sunday, they encountered a milling group of students at the Dormitory entrance, who all called each other Al. The group blindfolded Feikema and De Bie, made them sing a wavering duet, and ordered Feikema to strip to the waist, after which they painted a huge red F on his back, which they later covered with paper. He was then told to dress. The two novitiates were escorted to the Hekman Seminary Building then being constructed. The students took a ladder and made the two climb to the second story and left them in its midnight blackness. As they removed the ladder, they tossed up a book of matches.

Though the college had always been sternly against hazing, there were surreptitious forms of it, never violent but sometimes mean, such as dumping a freshman from South Dakota out in the suburbs in the dead of night to find his way home. To provide a viable substitute for such activities, the college for years had the "Soup-Bowl," an afternoon of fun and frolic and an evening party. As students grew more sophisticated, the "Soup-Bowl" was refined into an evening concert and finally abandoned.

No account of disciplinary activity at Calvin would be complete without mention of "Moses," his history, destruction, destroyer, and rehabilitation. In 1925 the last preparatory class gave the college a replica of Michelangelo's "Moses." This statue, in the front hall of the administration building, drew pranks like a magnet. He had an enormous wardrobe—hats, caps, berets, shawls, coats, mittens in great variety and color. He was a heavy cigar smoker. Pencil on one ear, cigar in mouth, jaunty cap on his head, he was a charming fellow. He took occasional trips around campus, went out for air now and then, and occasionally greeted the Curatorium. He would take in a basketball game now and then, zealously guarded by solidly built students. His mysterious ways were a great annoyance to Dr. Peter Hoekstra, a particularly tough questioner on the Discipline Committee. The fierce loyalties of the students to this statue as well as their disturbing antics with it came finally to a head at a faculty banquet at which Dr. Hoekstra's retirement was honored. What happened there is still inexplicable.

Professor Hoekstra was dignified, precise, authoritarian, and demanding as a teacher. He was remorseless in pursuing and unsettling the slothful. He was a very substantial scholar; he taught the good student to master detail and to buttress generalization with solid evidence. He was no expert in trivia, no pedant. He abhorred vagueness and he gave real insights. His dry, ironic wit did not spare oafs. If you were lazy, he made you feel ashamed; if you were stupid, he did not mark on effort. His assessments and interpretations were stimulating. He served the faculty for many years as a secretary whose minutes were impeccably accurate, and as a member of the Discipline Committee, where his grilling could be called ungentle. Beneath the dignity and slight aloofness was a kindly heart and his unheralded good deeds were many.

In 1954, as Dr. Hoekstra was being honored upon retirement, someone brought the statue of Moses ceremoniously up to his chair. Someone else in a humorous gesture brought up a large meat cleaver. His face grew red, and he impulsively picked up the meat cleaver and hacked the statue to pieces. Various pieces bumped onto the floor in an ominous quiet. Nobody expected this; I don't think he did. Possibly all the tensions of years of rugged disciplinary action found here an inappropriate outlet. The meeting ended gloomily. My wife and I took an arm of the statue home, one of the few solid pieces remaining. Later, apologies were made and all faculty members felt sorry for an admired and highly respected colleague. A replica of the statue was later made; it was kept in hiding and appeared only on rare occasions at basketball games, upon which almost invariably an unpleasant ruckus ensued, sometimes a minor riot. Finally, the legend

President Johannes Broene.

lost its interest, and Moses is at peace somewhere.

As the twenties drew to a close the faculty that was to exercise great influence on the future of Calvin had been strengthened by the appointment of Lambert J. Flokstra, whose brilliant mind gave depth to the Department of Education, Edwin Y. Monsma, who spent years mediating the problems pressed by evolutionary thought, and Miss Johanna Timmer, first dean of women and meticulous teacher of English. Already well-established were James Nieuwdorp, a witty man and a gifted mathematician, Albert E. Broene, teacher of Modern Languages, who gave thorough courses without orating or committing an outburst, usually riveted to his chair, from which he leaned back to write on the blackboard. His dry humor punctuated the drill in participles. Professors Stob and Ryskamp were highly respected teachers who rose to prominent positions in the college later, and J. P. Van Haitsma stimulated many first-rate students in biology. During these years, Professor Harry Dekker had begun his long service as registrar, at first simultaneously teaching chemistry. He literally spent himself in service to the college, often buried in work and taking on more. He was an extraordinarily kindly man, and I am sure the number of students and faculty whom he helped in various ways is extremely large.

The college had grown slowly from 325 students in 1925 to 335 in 1929. In 1930 it was ready for acceptance by the North Central Association of Colleges, an achievement fairly associated with the administration of J. Broene, who terminated his service as president in the spring of 1930 to return to teaching. He was a reluctant but quietly effective president who adequately met the mood and need of the times. He probably sensed clearly the emerging criticism of the college, and, although a man of deep convictions, he disliked controversy and could not be aggressive.

President Broene did not enjoy his high office; but he did enjoy teaching, and he was a superlative teacher. I think he could have taught just about anybody anything, and in the course of his career he almost did. He once said in class that he enjoyed teaching so much that he almost felt as if he should pay the Board instead of vice-versa. This seemed to me a bit of euphoria, but that he did enjoy it was obvious. Yet he was in no sense an exhibitionist, though he knew how to arouse interest through dramatic pictures. He was in every way, as a student perceptively put it, "an elegant gentleman," elegant in dress, diction, and decorum. Mildly spoken, gracious, and quietly friendly, he led by attraction. His imagination and sympathy, developed and tempered by great personal sorrows and abiding faith, enabled him to make great personalities of the past rise out of their books and walk before us. Widely read in literature, psychology, and history, as well as philosophy, he enriched his lectures with telling quotations and allusions. He was a master of a quiet, fresh, and lucid prose; he had the great gift of sounding good whether he was really saying something important or not. He was a memorable teacher without memorable eccentricities. If he had a fault it lay in an occasional tendency to elaborate a point beyond reasonable need. He once spent a considerable time on discussing the proper response to a lad who wants "to go out." What alternatives are there? Occasionally, also, he overdeveloped the parabolic example of his dog. But those little things made him human. Highly esteemed by colleagues and greatly admired by the vast majority of students, he was a man to remember, whose deep faith permeated his learning and contributed to the development of both in his students.

Calvin College could not escape the jarring effects of the twenties; neither devout training in home, church, and school, nor provincial isolation, ethnic separateness, or dedicated teaching could immunize it from

> *This strange disease of modern life,*
> *With its sick hurry, its divided aims,*
> *Its heads o'ertaxed; its palsied hearts.*

The doctrine of the antithesis was pervasively present, explicitly or implicitly. It is one thing to assert a difference in origin, nature, and destiny between members of the Kingdom of God and those of the Kingdom of this world. It is another matter to point out definitively the proper relationships between the two kingdoms, to develop a unified view of their relations, to integrate faith and learning. This integration became a prominent concern in the next decades. The stern Synodical decisions on worldly amusements prompted theoretical and practical dissent. Did the antithesis imply that seeing a good movie was sin? How about reading Plato and Hardy? How should the latter be done? As the tide of modernity rolled over the campus, it seemed to become an "estranging sea" between college and constituency. The problems of integration engendered a series of disputes and confrontations that came to a crisis in the thirties.

Some readers may regard references to Calvin's struggle in defining its relation to the world and worldliness as repetitive. The repetition is deliberate; the problems have recurred because they rise inescapably from trying to determine the way those whom Christ sought, found, and delivered should now travel in the world. For many Reformed believers the way clearly lies in the conquest of culture, in making its finest fruits subservient to the cause of Christ. But to some this way is fraught with peril; the choicest booths of Vanity Fair, whether in art, literature, or philosophy, are best avoided, and if they need to be examined, the paramount purpose of such examination should be condemnatory. The latter view, however sincere its exponents, smothers scholarship and misinterprets piety. Calvin can flourish only by nourishing both. As B. K. Kuiper said long ago in *De Wachter,* "You may not separate these two or put them against each other. When you do, you are departing from the true Reformed way and wandering off to the Anabaptistic." Calvin's ability to integrate faith and learning has always been on the line; it will always be unless either dimension of its ideal attenuates.

CHAPTER FOUR

HARD TIMES AT THE COLLEGE

The glitter and the gold that many Americans enjoyed and over-valued during the twenties lessened toward their end and on Friday, October 29, 1929, all but vanished as the stock market catastrophically tumbled. Millionaires and milliners, playboys and prophets, financial wizards and farmers shared the same fate. The big boom was over and elite stocks turned into wastepaper. The big bonanza became the big bust. Many a solid citizen lost his job, his car, his home. Relief lines grew longer and the soup kitchens were crowded. The garbage cans behind the imperial hotels were patronized by the poor who shoved aside the dogs. Passenger trains emptied and boxcars filled up. In 1933 over thirty percent of the labor force was unemployed. Banks went broke all over the country. Not until the beginning of World War II, twelve years after the dark October of 1929, did the country really turn the corner, and it took a new catastrophe to do it. During these years many American institutions were radically changed as the government played an increasing role in the daily life of all Americans. These were hard and gloomy years which Calvin did not escape.

The impact of the Depression was hardly felt during Broene's administration, but when the Reverend Mr. Rinck B. Kuiper took office in the fall of 1930, the long shadows of a darkening day were beginning to move over the campus. From the time he assumed office until he resigned in 1933, the economic news was all bad, and decreasing income meant one mournful retrenchment after another. Calvin suffered in the Depression, but never so severely as many other Christian schools. The Depression wiped out Grundy College. Some grammar school teachers taught all eight grades for $30 a month. One school I knew of gave a contract to a teacher for $40 a month, then repudiated it when another teacher offered to teach for $39 a month. My wife was offered a position in Lucas, Michigan, for $28 a month. When she told Professor Van Zyl that she could not live on that, he said, "There's nothing to spend it on in Lucas."

President R. B. Kuiper.

At some schools teachers received part of their pay in plumbing and painting. One student at Grundy paid his tuition in milk and later in veal. The faculty at Calvin took successive voluntary cuts up to a maximum of forty percent of their pay. This, doubtless, was a decided inconvenience, but in the light of the foregoing, hardly catastrophic. But it is always difficult to be the herald of "voluntary" pay cuts and that lot fell to President Kuiper.

The students of the thirties also faced hard times in college and more hard times after graduation. Scholarships were almost non-existent; parental purses were light if not empty; jobs were hard to come by. The little pay earned during summer was not enough. Little jobs at the college and about town, economy in clothes and entertainment helped. The pay for these jobs was pitifully meagre, often ranging from a dollar to two dollars for a day's work. In fairness, one should add that you could buy three pounds of ground beef for a quarter, get a haircut for twenty-five cents, and see a forbidden movie for a dime. A melancholy mood overshadowed the future: Ph.D.'s without work; law school graduates clerking at Kroger's; A.B.'s manning elevators. Even in 1938, one out of every five youths was unemployed or on relief in C.C.C. camps. A little jingle reveals the mood:

> I sing in praise of college,
> Of M.A.'s and Ph.D.'s
> But in pursuit of knowledge
> We are starving by degrees.

In a world where corn sold for eight cents a bushel in Iowa and was often burned instead of coal, where teachers taught all eight grades plus doing the janitorial work for twenty-five to thirty dollars a month, where gifted men and women languished on relief, the future looked bleak and empty. College life had a sober and uneasy undertone, whatever mirth bubbled on the surface.

Fortunately for the college, enrollment did not decline. In 1930 there were 393 students; in 1933, possibly the worst year of the Depression, 340. Even this was more than in 1928. This fact was hardly the result of a passion for Calvinistic education, but rather the benign side effect of the inability of some students to attend the school of their choice. The percentage of students coming from Grand Rapids reached its highest point in the Depression; it has been dropping ever since.

In 1930 the Board, after consultation with the faculty, appointed the Reverend Mr. R. B. Kuiper, then pastor of the La Grave Avenue Christian Reformed Church, president. He assumed his new duties in the fall of that year. He was a graduate of Indiana University and Calvin Seminary. He was an unusually effective and influential clergyman as well as a sharp and interesting writer. A man of eminent common sense, blessed with a cheerful personality and a fine sense of humor, he combined distance and involvement, dignity and approachability in a rare way. Though a very strong personality, he was neither stiff nor unbending, and his relationships with the faculty during his brief tenure were cordial.

Despite the intimations of a coming depression, Kuiper's administration began on a hopeful note. In 1930 the North Central Association of Secondary Schools and Colleges had approved Calvin's program. There was time to consider carefully the suggestions of the association, but the faculty at that time did not assess the suitability of the curriculum itself for the unique goals of the college. There were jarring notes coming. The problems of the proper mediation of Reformed perspectives and subject matter were arousing increasing attention. Certain faculty members were strongly critical of others for assumed default in this matter. Some strong-minded Board members were responsive to such allegations, and tensions began to smolder. Student disregard, even open contempt, for the stringent regulations on amusements troubled the Board and constituency. Ill-founded skepticism about the Reformed character of the instruction of certain professors bred vocal dissent. Talk about junior colleges in various parts of the country aroused anxiety. Voluntary cuts and the grim mood of the country did not ease matters. Retrenchment does not spread geniality.

In 1932 the faculty urged President Kuiper to accept his reappointment, which he did, but in 1933 he could not resist an appointment in the Orthodox Presbyterian Seminary at Philadelphia. His feelings toward his work at Calvin were ambivalent as the following characteristic comment reveals:

> I got a real kick out of my work. That this statement admits of several interpretations I know. There are unpleasant kicks and pleasant. Of unpleasant kicks some are literal, some figurative, and paradoxical though it is, one may get a pleasant kick out of an unpleasant; that is, one may get a kick out of being kicked.

Doubtless, he enjoyed the prospect of teaching at the seminary, but he must have sensed the coming crisis at Calvin. Some of the critical faculty members seem to have had his ear, if not his support. He had had excellent relations with the faculty up to this time, and he may not have liked to see them imperilled. His enlightened common sense, wit, insight, spiritual force, and dynamic preaching are remembered with gratitude.

The Board of Trustees at this time wanted strong leadership in a distinct direction. They were irritated by student conduct; they were disturbed about the assumed unreformed teaching. To put it in harsher terms, they were troubled about worldliness and apostasy. Knowing their state of mind, the faculty had great difficulty in selecting a candidate for recommendation. They finally decided to present the name of Dean Rooks, largely, as Dean Ryskamp says, "because the members could not agree on any other name to present." The Board rejected the nomination. The faculty, after a very close vote, added the name of Dr. Ralph Stob to that of Dr. George Goris.

President Ralph Stob.

The Board promptly recommended Dr. Stob to the Synod, which appointed him as president, to begin his work in the fall of 1933.

Dr. Stob, who had been a highly stimulating and amiable teacher, intended to be a strong president in order to meet pressing problems with, as Dean Ryskamp says, "a determined attitude to deal with *all* aspects of school administration." The question that really confronted him, whether he realized it or not, was *how* to be a strong president. Would it be best achieved by arm-twisting, imperial behavior, or persuasion? Considering the character of his faculty, the latter would appear to have been best. It does not seem to have so appeared to him. He was most vitally interested in the critical attacks on the school. He was also amenable to hearing the hostile attack of some vocal members of the Executive Committee of the Board. This receptivity later led to direct investigation of the college by the Board and the Committee of Ten. The strong desire to meet the external hostile criticism of student opinion and action resulted in unpleasant encounter between the president and the Student Council. In his foreword to the *Prism* of 1934, entitled "Reconstruction," he asserts, "To reconstruction Calvin students are committed. 'Reformata reformanda,' said the fathers." The students, however, had, as we shall see, different ideas than he had about the nature of reform.

During the thirties, the student body was small and closely knit, and there was a good deal of student participation in extracurricular activities. There were eighteen flourishing clubs on the campus. In 1932-33, Calvin had one of its outstanding basketball teams, and in 1933-34 beat its arch rival, Hope, twice. The coach was then William Cornelisse; he had no faculty status and was pictured with the team. In 1935 a significant appointment affected the future of athletics at Calvin greatly. Mr. Albert Muyskens was appointed to the Department of Mathematics, to serve also as basketball coach. He was singularly successful. During his career as coach, his teams enjoyed a winning percentage of .700. He helped organize the Michigan-Ontario Collegiate Conference, and his teams won the basketball championship five times in the seven years of membership. In 1941 they won the All Sports Award in that league. Muyskens also initiated the Physical Education requirement for all freshman and sophomore students as well as an intramural sports program for all students. These were highly innovative moves at the time, as were the original strategies his teams deployed in basketball. He also championed women's athletics and coached the Knighties to many victories. He was an outstandingly amiable man and highly respected at the college and among sports fans.

Many other activities flourished. The A Cappella Choir began its long and distinguished career. In 1932, Thespians was organized to produce annually at least one play for wholesome public entertainment. *Chimes* and *Prism* both published occasional pieces by Manfred, who later bewailed his self-described outcast state at Calvin. Student orations remained excellent and began to turn a critical eye on economic problems. Students also began increasingly to comment on the affairs of the college, notably in the matter of amusement. Forty percent of the student body belonged to at least one club. The Soup-Bowl was still observed, a lively day in early fall with its athletic contests, tug-of-war through a drenching rush of water, and evening party. Movie attendance was not minimal, but drinking was. In fact the bookstore ran a fetching ad:

"Lager Beer"
What does it mean? Find out by
buying the Webster's Collegiate
Dictionary.

The notorious "Varnish Case" topped the pranks of the era. All seats in the classrooms were varnished! But in performing this stupid prank, the students left fingerprints as clear as footprints in fresh snow; so they had to confess, even though some were sons of folk high in the ecclesiastical hierarchy. The whole affair reflected unfavorably, as such things do, on the school rather than on the culprits.

The Calvin faculty had operated democratically in relation to the administration; Board rules and a faint lingering of status prevented a similar operation in the faculty itself. In the early years of the college an instructor could rise to the rank of professor after two years. As the faculty grew, teachers were no longer automatically promoted, and sometimes served three two-year terms before promotion. In 1923 the Board had ruled that only professors could attend faculty meetings, so that by 1936 men with six and even more years of experience were barred from these meetings. Such men as L. J. Flokstra, E. Y. Monsma, H. J. Wassink, and W. T. Radius were all excluded, even after teaching at Calvin four years or more. This was humiliating to them and deleterious to the college. On March 13, 1936, the Educational Policy Committee recommended that these be admitted to faculty meetings and that full professors or six-year appointees constitute a Faculty Senate, later called *Council*. The Faculty Council would invite the others when it so desired. Technically, these were then part of the faculty, but were excused when the "goodies" such as new courses, teaching loads, tenure, salaries, and pensions were discussed. Obviously, this was no improvement; it was embarrassing and annoying to be invited to leave just when your interests were to be discussed. Teaching loads—a most vital matter—were discussed only by the Faculty Senate. After several years of such unsatisfactory procedures, the Faculty Council met for the last time on February 28, 1940, and was formally abolished in 1946 when all members with the rank of instructor or above attended.

Faculty meetings have been a very significant fact in Calvin's history. Tedious routine has to be undergone, but highly articulate debate has also occurred and meaningful decisions made. Tensely dramatic moments, in which one hopes a recommendation will be approved or disapproved, have alternated with healing humor. Strong personalities have clashed with amenity forgotten; others have spent the hours in absorption. Formerly, when minutes were still read, a few could spot a comma splice by ear. Some impatiently nursed the query, "When do we start objecting?" Good leadership and intelligent participation have constructively moulded the nature and destiny of Calvin. When I first joined the faculty in 1945, the older members had their own chairs, which one trespassed with embarrassment. A young faculty member kept respectful silence for a year. At that time the initiate moved gingerly in the hierarchical structures. In later years this has changed enormously, and younger faculty members speak with ease, animation, and sizeable duration. Formerly also, many matters now decided in committees were colorfully debated by the entire faculty. Recommendation for entrance to the seminary was debated in doubtful cases with delightful frankness. Recommendations for scholarships were sometimes characterized by eloquent and partisan zeal. New courses were often subjected to intense scrutiny except in the case of advanced courses in physics, for obvious reasons. There are still lengthy debates, usually concerned with lengthy documents, some of them little books. An immense amount of intellectual effort has been devoted to both the documents and the discussions. A great deal of noble effort has been expended in faculty meetings to improve the quality of the college.

The faculty numbered twenty-five in 1935 and never rose beyond thirty in this decade. The diffusion of tension possible in a large faculty was lacking, and the mounting problems involved everyone. Already in the late twenties there had been unrest about spotty student observance of the rules on worldly amusements and an alleged deficiency in the teaching of certain faculty members. Opinions were expressed in *Chimes* which angered some Board members and supporters. Already in the late twenties an alumni letter by J. De Groot in the *Chimes* caused irritation. De Groot found in Ann Arbor a "greater breadth of outlook." He felt that Calvin's "sectarian origin and purpose, while not opprobrious in themselves, are unavoidably productive of an attitude of intellectual and spiritual intolerance." Calvin was inhospitable to independent thought, and a student will there find it impossible to carry on "absolutely impartial investigation." There will be no real sympathy for varied views, only the hope that the student will return to "the Reformed position" and "find that the best." The implicit notion of what Calvin ought then to be offended many readers.

In the early thirties similar pronouncements appeared. *Chimes* editorials appeared announcing that "the attitude of the status quo as the best possible for the institution is the attitude of the closed mind," that what students need is "the moral courage of expressing our attitudes" even at the peril of "acquiring unfavorable attitudes from the authorities." The attacks grew really animated when they touched the question of amusements. One student wrote, "I'm sick of having our faculty lay down a series of don'ts for us." An editorial written in 1934 refers contemptuously to a "series of synodical bulls" on amusements and the "offensive attitude of the church toward them." Youth, it goes on to say, must be allowed "to think its own way . . . . through these difficulties. What we need is a new revival of St. Paul's Christian freedom." These statements are mild compared to the vitriolic outbursts of the late sixties; students felt as strongly then but they had better manners.

It is time to look at the decisions that precipitated years of administrative anguish and unpleasant faculty involvement, decisions which expressed the mind of the church at the time and opposed a new mind that has on the question of worldly amusements at least largely displaced the old. These two minds about worldly amusements bulk large in the history of the church and Calvin College.

Already in June 1925 the Board was "deeply concerned about the danger of increasing worldliness among our students." The Board appointed a committee to confer with the faculty to intensify dissuasive tactics; if these fail, said the Board, "this committee shall notify the faculty that students who persist in the practices mentioned above, must be disciplined to the extent of being suspended, also if need be, expelled." It reiterated these directives in 1926.

The rules were unenforceable. Students would not tattle, and faculty members could not prowl around theater doors as private eyes. The rules were in the catalog—they were openly resisted. In 1936, *Chimes* reported the results of a poll taken from one hundred male students. The following results were far from funny to some of the authorities:

Gentlemen Prefer:	YES	NO
Girls who attend good shows	69	23
Girls who do not smoke	57	33
Girls who pet	83	6
Girls who dance	41	46
Girls who take an occasional drink	42	47
Girls with Van Andel's famous curves	92	

The tide of worldliness swept in unabated.

The Calvin faculty in 1937 advised the Board that the rules were unenforceable. The Board, not having to enforce them, found this amazing. In 1939 it insisted that all students "sign a pledge card on which they promise to uphold the rules mentioned in the Information Handbook." All the students who enrolled in the fall of 1939 had to sign such a card. After the faculty informed the Board that it considered such a pledge unwise, and after further discussion with the Committee of Ten, the Board in 1949 substituted for the signing of a pledge card a statement on the application blank by which the student affirmed his acceptance of the rules of the school. This sounds Jesuitical but somehow it helped, by implying, I suppose, that while the student agreed with the rules, he was not bound by promise to obey them.

The Synod of 1940 took a strong stand on worldly amusements, ordering the faculty to discipline students who broke the rules and to expel "all students who refuse to heed the admonition of the school authorities in this matter." The faculty was admonished to reiterate and reemphasize its warnings. The problem persisted for many years because it was insoluble through legislation. It did not lessen until Synod relaxed its stand on theater attendance. The attitude students had been expressing or struggling to express is found in Synod's directives to the churches in 1966 at the end of the pamphlet *The Church and the Film Arts.* Here Synod says that films are "a legitimate cultural medium to be used in the fulfillment of the cultural mandate." The problems then shifted to the identification of "legitimate" films, particularly in the case of films shown on Calvin's campus.

To some all the agony about worldliness may seem a tempest in a teapot. I think that would be a decidedly superficial understanding of a problem which goes to the heart of the Christian life. Is the Christian life to be lived according to rigid, external rules, or upon inner-directed commitment to Christ, which if it is truly sensitive to the Lord's commands and loyal to their keeping will be able to exercise responsible choice in a matter where responsible choice has become crucially important. That Christian students should have access to and learn to appreciate excellent films as well as excellent novels and poems is widely accepted today. That, however, they should exercise a Christ-centered critical judgment in their viewing is not as loudly proclaimed, that their loyalty to Christ should make them avoid some films or walk out in disgust is sometimes forgotten.

In addition to the problem of worldly amusements, which be-

Worldly Amusements

in the Light of Scripture

and

Decisions Taken by the Synod of the Christian Reformed Church.

A book of 64 pages, and cover, size 5x7½ inches.

This booklet contains a report in which is an exhaustive discussion of the entire problem of amusements in the light of fundamental ethical principles revealed in Scripture. Special attention is given to theater and movie attendance, games of chance, and dancing. This report was signed by the Revs. E. J. Tuuk, H. J. Kuiper, R. B. Kuiper, H. Schultze, and Mr. H. Hekman. Every member of the Christian Reformed Church should know the principles explained and the facts recorded in this booklet. In the past many consistories have given a copy to prospective communicants.

Price 25c postpaid; $2.50 per dozen

Order NOW

CHRISTIAN REFORMED PUBLISHING HOUSE

47 Jefferson, SE, Grand Rapids 2, Mich.

Don't go to the movies.

came increasingly troublesome in the dying days of Stob's administration, another major concern was intensifying, variously described as tepid application of Reformed principles, unreformed teaching, or even apostasy. Its most influential and vocal proponent was Dr. Clarence Bouma of Calvin Seminary and his most distinguished target, Dr. Jellema of the Department of Philosophy. Dr. Bouma and those sympathetic to him felt that Jellema's teaching was too much colored by the influence of Plato and Hegel and tended toward idealism in philosophy. A few of the students felt that he raised too many unanswered questions. The latter reaction, however, was minute compared to that of the majority of his students, who felt that Jellema's teaching deepened their faith and commitment to Christ. President Stob and some of his friends and colleagues shared the fractional suspicion, and Jellema's position became increasingly uncomfortable. In this development the entire college suffered.

The tension was aggravated by the small size of the faculty and the student body. Differences of opinion and celebrated influence could not be boxed off; their effects pervaded the school. Students overheard, and gossip and rumor spread malignantly. It seems impossible to escape the possibility of jealousy. I have heard colleagues of Jellema make comments hardly consonant with scrupulously spiritual concern. Even some of Jellema's gifted students would utilize his insights and ape his methods in raising questions in a colleague's class. I have seen this done with embarrassing consequences; even when I saw it done I thought how utterly unworthy it was of Jellema's own vocally appreciative attitude towards his colleagues. President Stob was cool and distant in the face of the criticisms that arose. When Jellema received an appointment from the University of Indiana, he accepted despite pleas from students, the majority of his colleagues, and many leaders in the church. The lack of favorable interest of President Stob and some of his friends was an important factor in his decision to leave. The college was to be deprived for many years of his profound gifts and stimulating presence.

President Stob, who had been an excellent and genial teacher of Greek, forgot the moderation and the geniality of his classroom manner after he assumed office. Doubtless out of high conviction, but with frequently hasty and dictatorial action, he proceeded to meet the criticisms of the Board and other leaders in the church. When the students circulated a questionnaire at chapel without asking his permission, he immediately confiscated the results. The dormitorians, always a cohesive and influential body, resented the strong disciplinary actions on amusements. At one time, while he visited the Dormitory, the students greeted him disrespectfully. Later they apologized. When Dr. Jellema had accepted the appointment to the University of Indiana, Stob at first attempted to cancel the chapel scheduled in his honor, though he later relented.

President Stob was a forceful, highly gifted man with tenaciously held convictions, sometimes excellent, sometimes oblique, and sometimes ineffectively shared. He wanted Calvin to be academically excellent, and during his administration worthy curricular changes were made. New course programs were introduced, serious attention was devoted to the recommendations of the North Central Association, and the academic structure of the divisions was reorganized and improved. Applicants for admission had to take an English-reading and psychological test in addition to the Minnesota Reading Test. An effective pension system was introduced. His mode of improving student obedience to the rules was unfortunate. His attitude toward the faculty was sometimes unconsidered. At one time he suddenly submitted a new design for a gymnasium to the faculty. He was greeted with resentful silence since the faculty was not accustomed to precipitous planning without consultation. He stressed the word "distinctive" but misread the conditions prerequisite to cooperative zeal for its realization.

Dr. Stob had been an exhilarating teacher and a congenial friend to the students before he became president. Dr. Radius said of him in a memorial article, "You learned Greek in his class and you had a wonderful time doing it." There was never any "intellectual posturing." Whether he preached or whether he taught, you learned something. He had the rare ability to make Greek exciting despite its difficulty and the inevitable drilling. He had a phenomenal memory, and I clearly remember how he would not forget particular errors of particular students until he had trained them away. He gave away insights in asides. His course in Greek Culture was greatly prized by many students, including myself. He had high ideals for Calvin, a mind of unusual caliber, great vigor and dedication. He suffered from tactlessness and overdrive. I knew a gifted freshman whose father had died. His mother could not support him at Calvin. He was told to go see the president. He went to his home, up the long steps, where the president opened the door and talked to him on the porch. After hearing his story he said in 1934, "What you have to do is get those rich farmers in .... to take up a collection for you." That was it!

Even as faculty uneasiness mounted, he was known to come into the faculty room and say, "I wonder how many of you guys will be here next year." He was a good golfer, but he would undertake to correct a golfer who was beating him. This tactlessness diminished his effectiveness at many points. All recognized his scholarly aptitudes and genuine achievements in teaching and writing; one need not mythologize his presidency to maintain them.

Dr. Stob was reappointed for a four-year term in 1935. Faculty support was phlegmatic. The Student Council, moreover, asked the president not to accept the reappointment and sent copies of their resolutions to the faculty and Board. He accepted the appointment anyway, and the tensions continued for the next years. The rules against worldly amusements, as I have said, proved impossible to enforce. Identification of offenders was a slippery matter and involved undignified procedures if it were to be effective. No faculty member would lurk about theater doors. Students would not tattle; they protested the rules. Chapel attendance also posed problems, and the spectacle of professors prowling around peering into lobbies and rest rooms was demeaning and impractical. The notorious "varnish case" previously mentioned irked many people and reflected unfavorably on the administration. Discipline involving the children of important members of the church proved highly embarrassing.

The question of President Stob's reappointment in 1939 aroused a number of painful experiences. The faculty's recommendation not to reappoint him was not "taken from any personal ill-will on the part of faculty members toward the president but from a desire to promote the interests of the college." They recognized that he had "labored hard and diligently" and had strongly "emphasized the Reformed character of the institution," but that certain weaknesses, namely, "want of tact" and "inability to inspire personal confidence" had weakened his efforts. Dr. Stob chose to defend himself before the Board claiming "a lack of constructive, brotherly criticism on the part of the faculty." He also stated that he thought the faculty put too high a premium on diplomacy. He requested the Board to make a thorough study of the matter. In its answer, the faculty adhered to its opinions, saying that it "had sought to promote the spiritual interests of the school." To the faculty response, Stob made an elaborate response, but in the end eighteen of the twenty-two faculty members refused to recommend him. The Board advised him to withdraw his name for renomination. This he did. The whole matter understandably affected him deeply in both mind and body. He was physically ill for much of the following year. In the fall he returned to the teaching of Greek, and some years later accepted an appointment in Calvin Seminary.

After President Stob resigned, an immediate nomination of candidates suitable to both Board and faculty proved impossible. Professor J. Broene very reluctantly accepted the office for one year only. The Board and Synod immediately put a heavy bale of problems on his back. In fact the pressure they put on the college in 1939-1940 was both unprecedented and unrepeated. The Synod of the church in its 1939 session had appointed a Committee of Ten, both clerical and lay, to discuss with the faculty, student attitudes toward the rules on amusements and to analyze the character of its Reformed teaching. This commiittee met first with the faculty as a whole, and then the faculty met individually with subcommittees. At the latter meetings frank discussion provoked frank wrath. In the end, however, milder minds prevailed and a measure of understanding was achieved.

In the fall of 1939 the Board asked each faculty member to prepare a syllabus for each of his subjects. Obviously, such a detailed assignment could not be quickly prepared, and the Board accepted the faculty's proposal that each faculty member submit a statement of the way in which he integrated the Reformed faith and the learning he taught. To this the Board agreed, and the results were edited by J. Broene and bound in a volume permissible to read but not to quote. It is a curious volume—in variety of tone, description of pedagogical procedure, philosophical perspective or its lack. Some replies tingle with pique and bristle with outraged sensibility. In effect they say, "I've been teaching here over a quarter of a century and now this." One terse document in effect tells the Board that its writer knows his business and the Board ought to know theirs. At the other pole is a detailed document wholly innocent of philosophical statement, informing the Board of all the activities the writer engineers in doing his job. One long report gives an elaborate outline of courses from the first period to the final examination. There are also several papers of very high quality that truly grapple with fundamental problems and provide valuable insights.

The Committee of Ten read the reports in 1946, and in their reply made a genuine effort to be fair. The report says, among other things:

> The syllabi show that the professors at least know in theory what are some of the fundamental principles bearing on their branches of study and teaching and how they can be brought out. On the whole we considered them very good, some were excellent. There were none that we considered unsatisfactory from the viewpoint of principle.

I call this judgment very fair in the sense of being generous, because a few of the reports in all justice can be considered not unsatisfactory only because they say nothing at all from "the viewpoint of principle." This was the end of the matter, although some dozen years later the faculty had again to publish a statement of faithfulness to basic principles.

In its final evaluation based on interviews and syllabi the Committee of Ten expresses a fear that the faculty overvalues scholarly reputation. It also cautions strongly against admitting students from other faiths. Finally, it admonishes faculty members to study at the Free University for advanced degrees.

As I read the yellowing pages of the final report of the Committee of Ten, I was oppressed by an almost eerie sense of the erosion of attitudes and concerns, of the unrecoverable religious sensibilities of another generation. I suppose the spiritual anxieties so sincerely expressed in these pages would be suffocatingly narrow to young people today. These men, many of them able, and some of them outstandingly able, were greatly worried about a "lack of genuine spirituality" in the college and especially in the student body. They saw, as they thought, abundant evidence of this in a serious lapse into worldliness, a surrender to the world, the flesh and the devil. What they abominated, many of our youth today participate in. Attending movies—any movie—playing cards, and dancing were to them obviously sin. Their actual solution to worldliness, namely, a properly focused, inner-directed commitment to "our Lord and Savior and an earnest endeavor to make our life in body and mind an offering of thanks to God" is wholly Christian. Many of our young people share this commitment today. What they do not share is a belief that a maze of legalistic regulations, an absolutistic condemnation of these amusements, or constant surveillance of student life will achieve these goals. Many of the imposed restraints have come down, but our basic responsibilities as Christians living in this world have not. A major challenge will now lie in maintaining the profound spiritual concern movingly expressed in these yellowing pages in a world that luxuriates in personal freedom and frequently produces films barbarous in character, in comparison with which the forbidden films of the twenties were innocence itself.

Although beginning its work with an almost inquisitorial temper, the Committee of Ten had softened its approach and had finished its work with an element of success. There were fruitful conversations between the Committee and the faculty; the faculty had reassessed and described its goals; and the distasteful "pledge card" was abandoned. In March 1940, however, the committee's irrepressible ardor for problem-solving expressed itself in the recommendation of Professor Henry Schultze as president—prior to consultation with the

President H. Schultze.

faculty! The Board recognized the mistake and asked the faculty to augment the nomination. They added the names of Dr. G. Heyns and Dr. George Goris. Professor Henry Schultze of Calvin Seminary was elected and he assumed office in the fall of 1941.

This was a happy appointment. Professor Schultze enjoyed high respect among faculty, students, and the church. His geniality, wit, original insights, and unassertive, low-keyed leadership were welcome to all. A new era was about to begin.

CHAPTER FIVE

A TIME OF WAR, A TIME OF PEACE

Pearl Harbor was still two years away when President Schultze took office in the fall of 1939; but the web of war was spreading wider and wider, and as Hitler crushed country after country, involvement seemed inevitable. The omens of war, the fact of war, and the results of war affected Calvin deeply. The uncertainty about involvement coupled with a fear of its inevitability disquieted the minds of the students and jeopardized both study and planning. Then came Pearl Harbor on December 7, 1941, and the drums, as Whitman says:

Through the windows—through doors burst like a ruthless force
Into the solemn church. . . .
Into the school where the scholar is studying.

Calvin was faced with empty seats, sad casualties, and lamented deaths.

The war affected all aspects of Calvin's life. As boys left and few entered, the girls became a decided majority of the student body. Sixty-seven percent of the students in 1943 were women. In 1944 the girls took over the tradition-laden rooms and halls of the Dormitory. The number of courses offered gradually dropped. The *Chimes* was dominated by women, both as gifted editors and competent contributors. Faculty members Henry Zylstra, Henry Stob, and Harold Dekker joined the Armed Services. Athletics was numbed. But although college activities were slowed, they never stopped; the clubs, musical organizations, and athletic teams continued. The "Calvin Fight Song" and "Calvin Friendship Song" were regularly sung. Students participated actively in the drives for war loans. In one such drive the Calvin Volunteers, led by Dick Van Halsema's band, canvassed the neighborhood, selling bonds of every description. The drive made the front page of *The Grand Rapids Press*, a reaction utterly different from that in *The Tradesman*, a Grand Rapids paper which violently attacked Calvin for being pro-German in World

*The campus in 1946. Three-fourths of its buildings
donated by four families.*

Prof. H. G. Dekker and a full house.

The crowded chapel 1946.

Dr. H. H. Meeter and a fraction of his four hundred students.

WAA mess hall now serving knowledge.

War I. Soldiers were constantly visiting the college, from whence they and their friends went to the Bee Hive, where "You never (well hardly ever) get stung." Henry De Wit sent a perky letter from "A Hut in Iceland, five hours ahead of you." College life went on, but there was emptiness, solemn thought, loneliness, and a desperate listening for a lonesome drum.

President Schultze's administration up to the fall of 1946 was largely a holding period. In it, however, general good will was restored among faculty members and the Board. The president could describe the Board meeting in June of 1945 as "very harmonious." Relations between the student body and the faculty were cordial. This spirit of good will was exceedingly important as the strains of the dramatic burst in enrollment in the fall of 1946 produced a great deal of inconvenience, even discomfort. An enormous part of the concern of the college during the next years was devoted to providing accommodations, sometimes primitive. Calvin College, its buildings and staff of twenty-two, could serve 500 students well. In the spring of 1946 there were 503 students; in the fall of the same year there were 1,245; in the fall of 1947, 1,394. There was no magician's wand to make buildings rise to music; instead there was overcrowding. In 1947 *The Banner* featured a dramatic series of photographs illustrating the jammed classrooms. Student traffic in the halls, inching along like molasses, the packed chapels, 300 students in the laboratories operating in shifts since the facilities were suited to only sixty-four, 106 engineering students bottled up in space for forty, 780 men students spying out living quarters, only a fraction of the women occupying dormitory housing, an outgrown library, and an army mess hall for some classes. The oversized classes, unsatisfactory opportunities for study and recreation, the tightness everywhere threatened the morale of the college. Calvin needed a million dollars for expansion, and through the generosity of its supporters and the energy of a mass of workers, it was more than raised; in a few years an imposing Science Building and a commodious Commons were constructed.

Calvin needed a million dollars. In the week of November 10, 1947, Calvin Week was inaugurated to raise what was a truly huge sum at the time. Six thousand dedicated workers responded and presented a plan to many thousands more to give a dollar a month for three years. The families in the Christian Reformed Church and other friends of Calvin gave magnificently, and Mr. J. Van't Hof, chairman of the campaign, was able to present the Reverend Mr.

John Gritter, president of the Board of Trustees, and a long devoted friend of the college, a check for $1,000,000. A reconstructed army mess hall was erected just west of the Dormitory to house the Science Department until a fine, new building was complete. Here also the Music Department found room. Its practice sessions in the Main Building, while necessary and doubtless euphonious, had caused professors to cancel classes, and in one case drove a professor to such distraction that he refused to return till the competition was gone. Even Richard Tiemersma's eloquent adaptation of Tennyson's "Charge of the Light Brigade" failed to assuage his ire; the musicians moved. Later on, a spacious wing to the library was added in addition to the buildings previously mentioned. All buildings served to ease congestion greatly; the motto of the campaign, "Forward in Faith," had received God's rich blessing.

Housing proved hard to get—any housing. The most notable example of wholly unsatisfactory quarters was the "Alexander Lodge," a bland euphemism for disaster. It suggests a retreat for millionaires; it was in fact an unadorned and dilapidated group of schoolrooms condemned as unsafe for children. Here those who had just helped save the world for democracy reentered the barracks. Double-decked bunks (war surplus) were arranged to accommodate twelve students per schoolroom. There were no closets, bureaus, drawers. Coatracks were hung in nails driven into the frames around the blackboards. Each student had two lockers about eighteen inches wide to hold his personal effects. Footlockers, possessed by the prescient, might be kept. There were neither showers nor bathtubs; lavatories were wholly inadequate and toilets frequently were unobtainable. If you wanted a shower, you went to the Dormitory gymnasium a half mile away. One went to the same building for meals, where facilities to serve seventy students now had to serve hundreds more. Studying in the sleeping rooms was impossible; the classroom designed for study was equipped with long tables and chairs. Since twenty-five students used it, privacy was impossible.

It was indeed a spartan existence. Recreational facilities were limited to an old pool table and a piano invitingly placed in a draughty hallway. Smoking was forbidden but indulged in. Many faculty members made unusual efforts to entertain the students, but interests were often dissimilar. Professor A. E. Broene and his wife served as mentors in a benign fashion, but the actual discipline was enforced, when necessary, by the occupants themselves. Much good fellowship was enjoyed, but those who could find lodging in private homes left as soon as they legally could. The "Alexander Lodge" itself had a short life.

It is fitting here to insert a tribute to the services of the faculty wives in aiding and entertaining not only the students in Alexander Lodge but many others. For the Lodge and its members not only meals and friendship were offered, but also furniture, not always decrepit and unattractive. Throughout the years faculty wives have served the interests of students in a great many ways. I often wonder whether these kindnesses are remembered. They were done out of affection, concern, and good will. There was nothing about it in the contract.

The veterans were among the finest groups of young men Calvin teachers ever taught. Schooled in hard discipline, far-ranging in experience, mature in attitude, eager to redeem the time, they introduced a dynamic atmosphere of intellectual and spiritual concern. They brought to the college a strong faith, toughened by extraordinary stress and peril. Some of them still bore the results of these strains. One of my students had been a prisoner of war in Germany. He had survived on a diet of bits of mouldy black bread and reeking potato soup. He had to march day after day on this diet. Water he got from ditches and from patches of snow in open fields. When he went too slowly he was nipped by German police dogs. Finally, totally exhausted, he was dumped in a ditch for dead. He was later rescued by British prisoners of war but remained unconscious for fourteen hours. He recovered very slowly, and even now, at home and among friends, he was ill at ease and often bewildered. The nervous aftermath of the war was apparent also in other young men, but the majority outgrew it and responded energetically to their new opportunities. They not only did good work, but many had a genuine, scholarly interest in Calvinism and in properly integrating their studies with the Reformed faith.

Although the veterans were in almost all ways a decided asset to the college, their presence did not, understandably, ease the problem of worldly amusements. Most were in their twenties and felt they were mature enough to make their own decisions on these matters; their dates agreed. Movie attendance was widespread and openly discussed. Another matter under dispute was required class attendance. It sounded too much like the army. Some faculty members insisted upon assuring attendance through severe penalties; some attempted to secure it through interest; some seemed indifferent. The majority of the faculty succeeded in passing a tough rule on class

attendance. The *Chimes* responded by asserting that students skipped classes because they were dull and the notes could be shared, and that the only answer lay in a more stimulating classroom performance. This sounds wise unless one is teaching dangling participles or the German past perfect subjunctive.

The Calvin faculty had grown very slowly from sixteen in 1919 to twenty-two in 1945. In 1945 two faculty members were added; in 1947 five more. In the fifties and sixties the pace accelerated. More than once a dozen or more faculty members were appointed in a year. In one year nineteen were appointed. During the forties and fifties difficulties were encountered because candidates were scarce; in the sixties difficulties arose because available candidates had a multiplicity of choices. In the seventies, some fields offered a plethora of able candidates who were not needed. As the faculty grew the loose departmental relationship had to be tightened.

In 1949 the academic structure was reorganized. This reorganization clarified the precise function of departmental chairman and the nature of required departmental meetings. As the departments grew in size, the traditional informal discussion of courses grew impossible, and the departmental chairmen now had the sometimes onerous duty of assigning specific loads and courses. The machinery for the introduction of new courses was refined to insure the establishment of courses ministering to genuine needs in the college rather than to particular interests of professors. New courses were introduced with considerable care, and the introduction of new departments in the Arts and Languages engendered considerable discussion and fervid debate. A good deal of effort was devoted to foreign-language requirements, and a five-year nursing course was introduced. The faculty has operated under this organization until the time of this writing.

The faculty, as we saw in the last chapter, had been much concerned with the relationship between faith and learning. During the Schultze administration the word *integration* became increasingly dominant in the classroom and the publications of the college. In the October 1944 issue of *Chimes,* President Schultze published a leading editorial entitled "Integrative Education." Education at Calvin, he states, is "neither pupil-centered nor teacher-centered. It claims to be God-centered." Integrative education attempts to establish a proper relation to God in a fallen world; it attempts "to integrate the whole and the details of knowledge as God would have them integrated." This editorial, terse though it is, set the spiritual

tone and defined the intellectual endeavor of the college for many years.

The phrase "integrated education" may not be a happy one, as President Spoelhof suggests in his foreword to the pamphlet "Integrated Education" published in 1962, but if rightly understood, adequately describes an arduous grappling with complex problems over many years. President Spoelhof suggests that the phrase "carries with it too much the hint of a mechanical application." This is true, and sometimes it truly describes what was done; but when done rightly, when, in Dr. Spoelhof's words, there is "an organic, dynamic union of Christian faith with the life of the mind," then the phrase is highly significant. Calvin's teachers and some of its students, including many of the best of its students, were zealous in this respect. In 1961-62, chairmen of the various departments attempted to popularize their efforts in a series of articles in *The Banner,* later published as a separate pamphlet.

The pamphlet emphasizes that Christian higher education in Calvin College attempts an integration which is both thoroughly respectable by scientific or scholarly standards and thoroughly Calvinistic in applying Reformed perspectives to an interpretation and evaluation of sound learning. None of the contributors found the task easy or advocated a lifeless, slide-rule kind of critical appraisal. All emphasize the need for zealous commitment to Reformed principles in an educational enterprise academically sound and vibrantly Christian.

"Integrated Education" in the late forties and the fifties became a genuine interest of some of the most gifted students at Calvin. Norman Tanis, editor of *Chimes,* wrote about "the need of a dynamic Calvinism." "It is," he says, "our duty to assert, refine, and strengthen Calvinism." A group of able students wrote similarly in *Chimes,* and also used the Piet Hein press to disseminate their ideas. They published a symposium on literature and an anthology of *Chimes* editorials. Abraham Kuyper's *Christianity and the Class Struggle* was translated by Bernard Pekelder and Dirk Jellema and published by the Piet Hein press in 1951. The widespread interest in the poetry and spiritual odyssey of T. S. Eliot testifies to a deep religious concern. The literary clubs of this era were greatly interested in seeking Christian foundations for literary judgment. The ideas of the Christian faith were interwoven with a sturdy, reasoned attempt to relate Reformed perspectives to the culture in books and life. One never

felt that their tradition and religious roots were useless baggage to them.

Four important events following the end of the war proved highly significant in stimulating creative integration. They were the return of Dr. Henry Stob to the Philosophy Department in 1946, after his service in the war; the return of Dr. William Harry Jellema in 1947 to the same department, after teaching at the University of Indiana; the organization of the Calvin Foundation in 1948; the establishment of increased provisions for leaves of absence to be devoted to scholarly work.

Dr. Henry Stob, though usually associated with Calvin Seminary, served the college with distinction for many years. Students were greatly pleased as well as benefitted by his elegant diction and minute precision, his intellectual scope and his grasp of the history of fundamental philosophical problems and the varied answers given to them. He knew how to raise the key problems: How are faith and reason to be related? How are we to think about God? What is the possibility of a Christian philosophy? His gentle manner did not exclude tough requirements. He was genuinely interested in people and their common problems as well as in their ideas. His manifest Christian commitment influenced his students greatly. He served the Educational Policy Committee with analysis and suggestions while still at Calvin; he became one of the pioneering organizers of *The Reformed Journal,* a magazine to which he has given much of his thought and his life.

In 1947, Calvin's burgeoning enrollment demanded the appointment of a second member to the Philosophy Department. Dr. Jellema was at the time acting chairman of the Philosophy Department of the University of Indiana. After fruitful discussion with some of his former critics, including Dr. C. Bouma, Dr. Jellema accepted the appointment to the unanimous welcome of his colleagues. He returned in the fall of 1947 and enriched the college not only by his uniquely dynamic teaching, but also by his creative counsel in the Educational Policy Committee and his profound concern about the curriculum, a concern which culminated in the publication of his little book *The Curriculum in a Liberal Arts College.* This book was a milestone on the way to the massive reexamination of the curriculum in 1963.

The Calvin Foundation was organized in 1948 with an initial gift of $10,000 by Wm. B. Eerdmans, Sr., a Calvin alumnus. The Calvin Foundation was interested in "The development, enrichment and effective dissemination of Calvinism and the reaffirmation of Calvinism as a dynamic voice in the contemporary world." To implement this objective, the Foundation sought "to provide opportunity and tools" for scholarly activity, to promote artistic production, to enrich the Calvin community by supporting fellowship with spiritually similar groups. In the course of time such distinguished scholars as Dr. G. C. Berkouwer, Dr. J. Waterink, Reverend L. Verduin, and Dr. F. F. Bruce were brought to the campus for lectures and discussions. The Foundation has sponsored many other worthwhile projects.

The number of non-Christian Reformed students at Calvin has never been large. Even in 1974-75, after extensive advertising and active recruitment, the number was only fifteen percent of the student body. In the thirties the Board expressed grave misgivings about broadening the admissions policy. Dr. Henry Beets in *The Yearbook* of the Christian Reformed Church writes in 1936:

> A considerable number of students at present come from other circles than our own, an encouraging testimony to Calvin's reputation, but also constituting both a problem and a challenge. May God give wisdom to solve the problem and take up the challenge in the very best way.

Many of the faculty have felt that Calvin was limiting the range of its witness through such misgivings and depriving itself of admirable students. Students from sister churches such as the Reformed, Protestant Reformed, and Orthodox Presbyterian have always been welcome. Students of attested Christian commitment from other denominations have also been granted admission. But it was undeniable that Calvin also had something to say to students not yet committed to Christianity but sincerely interested in Calvin's witness. In one facet of its academic life, Calvin had already been reaching out for many years, and the generally favorable impact of this work suggested that widening the admissions policy might be very desirable. This facet of Calvin's life was the summer school program. After considerable discussion the faculty and the Board widened the criteria for admission so that at present, according to the catalog, "Students who are interested in the Christian atmosphere and curriculum at Calvin and show an interest in its aims are eligible for admission." The faculty now have an opportunity to share their Reformed convictions with students who have expressed a genuine interest in them.

Calvin's initial leap in enrollment in 1946 was due to the admission of hundreds of veterans. There was also a very noticeable increased registration of high school graduates. A clear and accelerating trend had begun in the country to provide a college education for all young citizens who desired it. The country seemed on the road to mandatory availability of college education for high school graduates. This prospect proved disturbing to many college teachers. Dr. W. T. Radius, in an article in *The Calvin Forum* of February 1949, presents an incisive statement of the problem. Granting that universal college education may be very costly but not financially unrealistic, he goes on to say:

> The plain and unpleasant truth which we must face is this, that the presence on the college campus of everybody's son and daughter will work havoc with the educational standards of the colleges.

If college education is democratized, its excellence will be attenuated. "Colleges," said Radius, "already have had to adjust their standards to the level of entering high school graduates." If colleges continue this process, the education they give will fail the requirements for leadership in this country. If it should occur at Calvin College, it may compromise "the *intellectual* standards of our denominational college." Such standards cannot be dissociated from our Calvinistic witness, which demands "intellectual integrity." Dr. Radius concludes his article by calling for a varied curriculum if all are to enter college: "To expose all of them to the same curriculum can only result in frustration for many and mediocrity for all."

Admission standards at Calvin have been a subject of much debate. How much does Calvin owe to the mediocre student whose parents have loyally supported the college for many years? Is it any answer to admit with generosity and then to flunk hard-heartedly? Should special remedial programs be encouraged? Should tough courses be diluted or excised? Should we remove the hard and later the soft languages from the requirements? Should we deescalate the marking system? If hard times come, should we be even gentler? Should we take on a whole new program of consumer-oriented courses? Should we give a greater variety of degrees? Such difficult questions have demanded hard thinking by the administration and faculty. The answers both have given to these complex problems have preserved Calvin's reputation as an excellent liberal arts college, though severe tests of the academic integrity of the college lie ahead.

In such concerns as the foregoing, as well as in many others,
Dr. W. T. Radius, Professor of Classical Languages at Calvin from
1934 to 1972, played a commanding role. Combining wit and erudi-
tion, unusual insight with wide interests and sympathetic concern,
he was an outstanding teacher who could say, "Now, I tell you—
it's this way," to his students with complete acceptance. He wisely
sponsored many student activities and served admirably on important
committees. A gifted and stimulating writer, he contributed to various
journals, and in the last years he and his wife have written many
artistic and deservedly popular articles in *The Banner*. He edited a
textbook of selections from Lactantius. As a teacher of Greek and of
classical history, he made marked and abiding contributions to the
lives of his students and has had an immense influence on the intellectual development of the Christian Reformed clergy. President
Spoelhof has often paid tribute to his invaluable private counsel.
His acute mind, wide knowledge, admirable balance, and personal
concern have enriched the lives of many of his colleagues.

Summer school at Calvin was introduced in 1940 at the request
of the Superintendent of the Grand Rapids Public Schools. The
State Code had just required all public school teachers to work
toward the acquisition of the A. B. degree. Many of these teachers
would find a summer session at Calvin highly desirable. Calvin
agreed to this service, which was offered on the top floor of what
was then Davis Technical High School and now is Grand Rapids
Junior College. There was no air conditioning, and the tar bubbled on
the roof outside of the room I taught in. Many of these students had
not been to school for years and found the work decidedly hard.
One man in my class, well in his fifties, had obviously not read a
book through in years. In addition, he was hard of hearing; even
his front seat was not too helpful. Fortunately, he taught typing.
One hundred and fifty students were enrolled. The attitude of the
students was generally splendid; they worked hard and many of them
did well in the end. The whole experience was highly affirmative,
and Calvin decided to retain the program. Later it proved especially
beneficial to veterans who wished to expedite their work and faculty members who sought to augment their pay. The Summer School
added another section and later two more so that today a student
can do a semester's work in a summer. Furthermore, the Summer
School convinced many faculty members that a wider witness to
students of various religious persuasions or even of no pronounced
religious persuasion bore fruit if not in changed convictions at least

in a more sympathetic attitude toward the Calvinistic principles of the college.

The student body during the second half of President Schultze's administration was decidedly atypical. The moral and spiritual qualities of the veterans, a highly influential segment of the student body, set the tone of college life. They were often honestly critical but never abrasively so. They tempered criticism with good sense and a spirit of cooperation. The war had also affected the nonveterans, expanding their horizons of concern and thought. Though they had not been brought face to face with the "great death," they had lived in its shadow for years. No one was somber, but seriousness in ideals and application was general. Their energies spilled over into many worthwhile extracurricular activities, which multiplied after the war. The Thespians were now giving three plays during the school year. The Music Department expanded its offerings, and an ensemble as well as the fine Veterans' Choir was organized. The *Chimes,* under editors C. Rensenbrink, R. Jellema, N. Wolterstorff, C. Ter Maat, N. Vos, R. Staal, Charles Orlebeke, and R. Jager, reached a new high level of responsible journalism, with incisive editorials, excellent book reviews, and notable feature articles. The increasingly independent stance of some of the editorials and the nature of some of the pieces in *The Literary Review,* established in 1949, raised questions the next administration would have to deal with. The *Prism* became a competent even luxurious volume, but was still restricted to college life. In later years *Prism* would greatly expand its concerns and pictures from the campus to the city and the countryside, from the traditional shots of students and faculty to photographs of barn doors, scarecrows, sleazy tenement houses, coffee pots, wasps, flies, abandoned outhouses, street signs, driftwood, various quarters of the moon, and visiting politicians. Charles Bult replaced Coach Muyskens as basketball coach, producing steadily improving teams, including the great team of 1951, whose 83-43 victory over Hope at the Civic Auditorium was one of Calvin's great moments in sports. Muyskens continued his success in producing some superb tennis teams. In 1951 the Calvin College "Alma Mater," still regularly sung at college activities, was published. The lyric was written by Celia Bruinooge and the music by Dale Grotenhuis.

The Discipline Committee is often busy. It is interesting and significant to note what it is busy with. In the twenties and thirties it had to deal with the thorny problems of worldliness, in the late sixties with the deeply disturbing problems of pot and drugs, and at all times with various, even ingenious, varieties of horseplay. In the late forties and throughout the fifties, understandably enough, parking violations were common, often disregarded, and protested. One banner week records seventeen violations. A traffic officer was appointed, and he performed his task with cheery mercilessness. Pranks of various kinds occurred. One student was apprehended after taking off the doorknobs from all the classrooms. Since he was in my class, I asked him to read with appropriate feeling these lines from Whitman:

> *Unscrew the locks from the doors!*
> *Unscrew the doors themselves from the jambs.*

Another student took pleasure in detonating thunderous dynamite explosions in Franklin Park. The most ingenious prank I saw at Calvin was the parking of a Model T Ford in the lobby of the Administration building. It was an amazing bit of dismantling and reconstruction. The most outlandish prank at Calvin was the mounting of an outhouse on the Commons Building.

The strangest case I ever encountered was a case of plagiarism, which deserves a paragraph of its own. Plagiarists do not often react according to conventional expectations. They are, of course, minor crooks, not inveterate criminals, and they hate to be caught. When they are, they have a bagful of excuses and in my experience few tears, little repentance, and a good deal of resentment. One boy told me he copied the passage because it stated the matter much better than he could, and since I was after good writing, he was providing it. The teacher has to have hard evidence, not always easily obtained. The strange case to which I have referred concerned a young man whom the hardest evidence obtainable could not break down even in the face of the ruthless pressure of the Discipline Committee, one of whose members, Dr. Peter Hoekstra, was no mean questioner. During the previous spring he had won a prize of $35 in the Eerdmans Literary Contest. During the summer a young lady who had returned to Lynden, Washington, discovered the identical poem, not a short one, in an anthology. None of the judges had been aware of the poem. We thought that the discovery amounted to completely convincing evidence, but the boy denied ever having seen the poem. Even when confronted by the fact that two poems of sixty lines, identical even to the punctuation, independently created by two different poets would be a psychological and literary happening of the first magnitude, he would not budge. His parents helped him not to budge. He refused to apologize, kept the $35, and left Calvin at the end of the semester. The last I heard of him was through an account in the newspaper. He had won a boat race.

After four years of hard and fruitful study, or genteel observation and economy of effort, or diligence, little ability and benign treatment, the student graduates. I have attended fifty-three commencements. Whether one enjoys them or not, they have to be held in a suitable place. Personally, I have always found them happy occasions. There are always fine students whom one is happy to honor and a few one is happy to escape. In the early days, commencement could almost have been held in Professor Boer's living room. Calvin's first public commencement was held in 1906 in the La Grave Avenue Christian Reformed Church. After that, commencements were held in various local churches. From 1917 to 1947 they were held in the Calvin Auditorium. For a time they were held in the Grand Rapids Civic Auditorium and then at the Calvin Fieldhouse. In 1948 colorful robes were introduced and this variety of robes has been generally enjoyed by the audience. For years Calvin College and Calvin Seminary held a double-header with one major speech and two shorter ones. Furthermore, since each graduate of both institutions was personally congratulated by each president as he marched across the platform, the program became interminable. So the exercises were separated. The college fieldhouse is now packed and the audience faces a colorful platform with banked flowers, dignitaries, and the symbolic departmental banners. The president now grants the degrees according to academic grouping, attended by appropriate comments to each. In recent years a litany has been read with appropriate portions for students, faculty, and audience.

President Schultze's administration was on the whole an era of good feeling and buoyant optimism. He was not a forceful administrator who held all the reins in a firm and unwavering hand. Sometimes the administrative set-up reminded one of a triumvirate in which the president, Dean Ryskamp, and Registrar Dekker exercised fluctuating bursts of power. The president was not a bulletin-sending man; some thought he did not send out bulletins enough; some, in fact, thought it was hard for him to determine the exact nature of the bulletin he did not care to send. He did not seem profoundly interested in academic matters. Devoid of all intellectual pretense and impatient of prima donnas, he deflated both with a sly and effective wit. His insights were abundant and original and his chapel speeches memorable for their informal effectiveness. There was something enigmatic about him; his friendliness was genuine but it was hedged in by reserve. A sparkling and interesting preacher, he enjoyed wide popularity and respect in the church. While conducting a service in the Fuller Avenue Christian Reformed Church, he suddenly became dazed and had to be helped from the pulpit and then taken to the hospital. He had suffered a slight stroke. He improved gradually, though the effects never wholly left him. Yet, even while recuperating, he cooperated with Acting President Henry Ryskamp.

On March 5, 1951, he startled the faculty by announcing his resignation. In a statement to the student body on Tuesday, March 6, he said among other things that the main reason for resignation lay in his continuing physical difficulty. He went on to say he was

> loath to take this step because of my pleasant associations with the institution and because I have given a large part of myself to Calvin. This step, which is a bit painful, is not lightly taken.

His words "I have given a large part of myself" were characteristically modest. He had guided the college through a time of unwieldy and almost uncontrollable expansion. When he became president in 1940, the faculty and administrative staff numbered twenty-two; when he resigned in 1951, it numbered forty-seven with nine assistants. The enrollment of 499 in 1940 had dropped to 385 but rose to 503 in 1945 and then to 1,270 in 1950. He never spared himself in helping to resolve the tangled problems of sudden growth. In addition he regularly wrote perceptive articles for *The Banner*, delivered many addresses, and preached many sermons. He was an unusually gifted man, especially in sharing uncommon insights in a popular way, and his devotion to the Kingdom inspired both his colleagues and the students.

CHAPTER SIX

THE YEARS OF CONFIDENCE

The Korean War, for which twenty Calvin students enlisted and others were recalled, seems a misty if not forgotten war today. The war was complex and vicious enough, but Eisenhower said, "I shall go to Korea" and that seemed enough. Dwight D. Eisenhower was elected in 1952 and the "I Like Ike" buttons reflected a worldwide sentiment. Despite racial violence in Little Rock, a storm over Suez, the rise of Castro, and the menace of McCarthy, there was little unrest in the country. The streets were quiet and dissent spoke in whispers. The decade of the fifties was one of growth, prosperity, and a huge investment in education. Money poured into college coffers on an unprecedented scale, and Calvin shared in the abundance.

The students of the fifties have often been called the "silent generation." If that implies that they were mindless or never used the minds they had, it is a wholly false notion, particularly at Calvin. Of course, they did not wear the later modish protest of faded blue jeans and crummy sweaters, neither did they lug big beards around or pile up their hair in miniature hay stacks, but though appearance was conventional their minds were keen and their intellectual assessments incisive. It would be more accurate to call the students at Calvin the "polite generation." They were as intelligent as any group of students I have taught, and in some ways they were better prepared for college than in recent years. The number of assistant-ships and scholarships that the best of them obtained would compare favorably with those of any era in Calvin's history. Any reader of *Chimes* in this era will have ample evidence of intellectual ability. The students were neither violent in action nor brash in expression. Obviously, I am speaking of the students who set the tone of college life; the genteel observers, those who say "an hour we have, ah, let us waste it well," are always with us.

What was striking then and even more so in retrospect is the spiritual concern, especially manifested in the attempt to integrate

105

President William Spoelhof.

faith and learning. In the "Foreword" to the *Prism* of 1950, edited
by C. Ter Maat, these words are found:

> We feel that Calvinism, far from being dead or dying, represents
> a segment of that orthodox Christianity which holds the hope
> of a world that needs salvation in blind alleys where no salvation
> is to be found.

The words are prophetic and this conviction energized many of the
ablest students during the next years. The concern was manifest in
the busy clubs of the day, the publications, and the classroom. It
was a major expression of the interest in *integration,* a dominant
word in these years.

President Schultze, who had piloted the college successfully
through the difficult years of war and the novel adjustments to peace,
was in the providence of God unable to lead in the promising era

to come. His resignation was deplored and answered, as we have noted, by deep appreciation.

Fortunately, the faculty, aware for some time of the president's health, had in 1950 adopted a procedure for presidential appointment. The faculty nominating committee included the Educational Policy Committee and five other members elected from the faculty. This committee prepared a tentative nomination. The choice was difficult because various members of this committee had themselves been suggested for this office by faculty polls. The committee presented the names of Dr. Henry Stob, Dr. George Goris, and Dr. George Stob to the faculty and, after receiving its approval, to the Board of Trustees. The Executive Committee of the Board replied that it "was ready to eliminate some names from the list of candidates" and requested faculty reaction to the name of Dr. William Spoelhof. The faculty approved the addition of this name to the list and then added a request to place the names of Dr. William Harry Jellema, Dr. Henry Ryskamp, Dr. Henry Zylstra, and the Reverend Mr. Peter Eldersveld on the list of candidates. The Board recommended Dr. Spoelhof and Dr. Henry Stob to Synod, and this body appointed Dr. Spoelhof as the president of Calvin College to begin his work in the fall of 1951. In September, President Spoelhof began the longest presidency in the history of the college.

President Spoelhof at the time of his appointment was the youngest of Calvin's presidents. He had been graduated from Calvin in 1931; then proved a highly successful teacher at the John Street Christian School in Kalamazoo and at the Oakdale Christian School in Grand Rapids. He served in the armed forces in the Netherlands on the staff of the Office of Strategic Command, where he became thoroughly acquainted with administrative detail and procedures. After the war he returned to the University of Michigan, where he received a Ph.D. in history. He taught in the History Department at Calvin until his appointment as president and also filled the position of president of the Alumni Association, where he served with vigor and distinction. He brought to the presidency a unique flair for the complexities of administration, a persuasive talent for public relations, a profound commitment to academic excellence, and the Reformed perspective which would foster and illumine it. He had the courage and imagination to envision long-range plans for the college, many of which through God's grace he saw fulfilled.

The college he was to serve was growing spectacularly. In 1940 it had a faculty and administrative staff of twenty-two and no emeriti. The student body numbered 499. In 1946 enrollment reached 1,245; in the fall of 1951 the student body numbered 1,470, and the faculty and administrative staff had grown to forty-seven with nine assistants. There were now nine emeriti. During the next seventeen years the college had no problem attracting students. The acquisition of an excellent staff, one of the president's early, primary, and continuing goals, was a recurring and in some cases a desperate problem. The horizons appeared unlimited and student enrollment did not begin to taper off until 1969. In certain departments, however, the need for qualified personnel is still a serious problem.

During the early years of this decade (1951-1961), Calvin was still a crowded world with slow lines inching ahead at many occasions, but the compression was greatly relieved by the attractive and spacious Science Building (1952) and the new Student Commons Building (1953), where the student lounge, perpetually occupied snack bar (except during chapel and that by fiat), and dining hall became the center of informal student activities. The size of the student body and the relatively reasonable cost of things permitted a cohesiveness among the student body which was weakened by size and price in later years. Of course haircuts were no longer twenty-five cents, turtleneck sweaters $1.25, and double-breasted suits $24.50, as they had been in the middle thirties, but banquets did not entail financial ruin and entertaining students in private homes through hospitality or for the convenience of clubs was not excessively expensive. The traditional Soup-Bowl, now called the Mixing-Bowl, was still in full flourish, as were club picnics. The girls' college halls were small enough to stimulate a sense of identity and pride, and even the Commons' dining hall remembered birthdays. Forensics still drew talented members and student support. The opportunities for musical expression were rapidly growing. The basketball team won fourteen out of eighteen games in 1952 and eighteen out of twenty-two games in 1954. Calvin entered the Michigan Intercollegiate Athletic Conference (MIAA) in 1953. The first MIAA event in which Calvin participated was a cross-country meet in which Calvin's team members were recruited from Coach Barney Steen's basketball prospects and Coach Dave Tuuk's track squad. Coach Steen's basketball squads tied or won the title during their first three years of participation, and Coach Tuuk's cross-country runners won six straight titles. His cross-country runners from 1958 to 1963 won thirty-nine straight league victories, a record still intact. The spirit of the school was affirmative in almost every way during this decade. There was one major, jarring exception to this statement, as we shall see later.

As a college grows larger, the individual tends to become anonymous in the sea of faces, and the student body tends to splinter into little groups. The entire student body never meets together; the chapel is too small to hold them; no college event ever attracts them all. In 1952 the Student Council recommended and implemented the idea of a Calvin Homecoming, an annual event that not only aroused a good deal of student participation, but also vitalized the loyalties of many alumni. The Homecoming Board arranged a very successful series of events in that year. The traditional queen and court were chosen; Calvin beat Hope before a jammed Civic Auditorium; more than 1100 wriggled their way to the Commons afterward, where alumni of years back recalled bright cheeks, slim bodies, pranks, friends, and achievements. In later years elaborate, ingenious, and laboriously built displays were constructed, and the exhausted students wobbled into early classes or simply stayed home and slept. Lectures by faculty members and visiting speakers drew solid and appreciative audiences for many years. Later, whether sadly or smugly, the queen and her court were abandoned as an archaic sentimentality and the displays were junked as juvenile. The *Chimes* pontifically said that the event "must not degenerate into a beauty contest." It was never that, and the queen and her court were a gracious and pleasant compliment to the college, and the displays often showed remarkable talent. Homecoming is still, however, a lively and worthwhile event and has done much to strengthen the loyalties of the alumni.

A student reflecting on Homecoming in *Chimes* states the event brings together many graduates, most of them ordinary people rather than celebrities, who have "helped many people in many ways, have passed on to others some of the things they have gained at Calvin," and "have attempted to satisfy the obligations incumbent upon them as graduates of Calvin." If Homecoming fosters such a spirit, it is eminently worth having.

During the years 1951-1962, the old pattern of extracurricular activities was still in full bloom. During the year 1956, there were eighteen clubs; in 1959, there were twenty-six, including six literary clubs. In fact literary clubs aroused so much interest that Professor Wyngaarden of the seminary called Henry Zylstra up late one evening to suggest that we have twenty-six literary clubs, one for every letter in the alphabet, including "X" I suppose. Both *Prism* and *Chimes* produced outstanding work during these years. Musical organizations included the very successful Meistersingers, the Radio Choir directed by Professor James De Jonge, which served The Back-to-God Hour with distinction, the Concert Band, the Orchestra as well as the A Cappella Choir and the Messiah Chorus. Baseball enjoyed a full season, with only eight losses. The varsity basketball team enjoyed the best season in college history up to this date, winning eighteen games and losing only two. Jim De Bie and Stan Koster broke school records in track and pole-vaulting. Professor John Vanden Berg won a smashing victory in the election for city commissioner in the third ward while the tennis team he coached tied for sixth place in the MIAA. Thespian productions under the leadership of Mrs. Ervina Boevé became one of the highlights of the school year. In 1959 visiting celebrities Dr. Herman Dooyeweerd and Governor "Soapy" Williams spoke on the campus, and in the words of *Prism*, "Some of the ideas stayed behind." The traditional pattern of extracurricular activities was in full midsummer pomp. In the early sixties they were still in autumnal bloom, but the winter of their discontent and demise was at hand.

Student attitudes toward the faculty were overwhelmingly favorable. The *Prism* of 1952 says of the current faculty:

> Because, then, of their Christian devotion, scholarly capability, and sympathetic understanding, we the students are sincerely proud of and humbly thankful for the fifty-seven members of the Calvin College Faculty.

That the vast majority of students shared this evaluation was abundantly clear through classroom reaction and private conversation. That some students and some influential elements in the church did not was equally clear in the protest seven students submitted to the Board in May of 1951 and in the *Petition* the Reverend Mr. H. J. Kuiper was circulating across the nation in 1952. Both documents were extremely critical of the college, and the protest of the seven students was violently critical of six members of the faculty. These documents, more fully described in the chapter "Little Foxes in the Vineyard," attack allegedly faulty integration of faith and learning at Calvin and voice the complaint "that there is no pronounced spiritual atmosphere in our college." Both attacks caused uneasiness and suspicion in the constituency, dismay in the faculty, and a tough and unpleasant problem for the new president. So great was the uneasiness that under President Spoelhof's leadership the faculty pre-

sented a necessary, highly affirmative, but somewhat mortifying statement to the Board of Trustees in May 1952. In it the faculty reaffirmed its genuine loyalty to the "absolute Lordship of Christ,"
the infallibility of Scripture, the authority of the historic Reformed
Creeds, and the reality of the antithesis. The Board received it with
"keen apprciation" and submitted it to the Synod of 1952. Since
the same Synod refused to acknowledge the *Petition* circulated by
the Reverend Mr. H. J. Kuiper and "deplored" the way it arrived at
Synod, the tension relaxed, although some members of the church
felt, in the words of one of them, that "The sugary words and
phrases used in the faculty statement while separating the flock from
their cash" were written to insure physical expansion. The Two Million Dollar Campaign for expansion approved by the Synod of 1952
under the motto "Forward in Faith" did not go forward as splen-
didly as the Million Dollar Campaign because some of Calvin's
former supporters lost faith in the college. Seven hundred and fifty
of the students, however, contributed the large sum of $34,341. Grad-
ually, confidence was restored and it was to be the dominant tone of
the fifties. President Spoelhof's remarkable ability to dampen angry
and often irresponsible explosions of criticism was clearly in evidence
throughout his handling of these hard problems.

Apart from these unsettling matters, there was a buoyancy in
the air, a decorum in the life-style and attitudes of students, an inti-
macy in the faculty, and a peacefulness in the neighborhood one looks
back to with nostalgia. Splendid new buildings enriched the campus;
those that were old were being attractively refurbished; new books
and magazines were filling the enlarged Hekman library. Student enrollment was growing every year. Faculty salaries edged steadily up-
ward and younger faculty members could cheerfully say with Brown-
ing: "Grow old along with me!/The best is yet to be." Students
then were neatly dressed, uniformly polite, almost deferential. President Schultze, a few years earlier, called a student into his office
for going to class in rolled up sleeves and said to him, "This may be
all right for factory work, but in college we dress like gentlemen."
Some years later when a student came into my class barefoot, I said
to him, "Now listen, Robinson Crusoe, you get your man Friday
to lace you up before you reappear." He had his shoes on at the next
class. In the late sixties, when the young men slouched in, amply
bearded like members of the Sanhedrin, and both young men and
young women pattered in bare feet, times had changed.

The faculty was small enough so that you were never embarrassed to have to introduce a colleague, vaguely familiar, but unknown to you by name. Twenty-fifth anniversaries, illnesses, farewell speeches had an emotional resonance impossible in a faculty triple its size. Even the neighborhood was quiet, relaxed—and safe. One could still walk home alone through Franklin (recently renamed Martin Luther King) Park after a late meeting at the college without fear of mugging. As I reflect on these years, I feel much as Blake did in recalling his youth even though the ages are different:

> Such, such were the joys
> When we, all girls and boys,
> In our youth time were seen
> On the echoing Green.

Despite the untoward incidents recounted, the new president inherited a "going thing": an appreciative student body, a cooperative faculty that soon held him in high regard, enthusiastic support in the Board and the church, and a surging enrollment. After his first year in office, the students dedicated the *Prism* to him and among other compliments stated that, "Looking back over his first year, we can only say, 'He's done a swell job.' " This general acceptance made the changes he had to introduce because of a constantly growing college smooth and palatable.

The changing road was further smoothed by the president's introduction of a Faculty and Board Conference in September. The first year the conference was held at Camp Geneva on Lake Michigan. It was a two-day retreat, and the austere beds and crowded cabins led to scant rest. I still remember Dr. Wyngaarden prowling around in full regalia with dangling watch chain at 3 a.m. Then for many years the conference was held at Castle Park, south of Holland, where the musty basement room lingers in memory with fine discussion and stimulating papers on subjects ranging from Calvin's image to the practical problems of censorship. As the faculty grew larger, the meetings were held in a larger hall under a baking tin roof. Later conferences were at St. Mary's Lake near Jackson. The last meeting was held at Calvin and, as had been the procedure for some years, lasted only one day. These conferences have provided a good deal of light, occasional heat, and rare dulness. The conferences stimulated solidarity in effort and spirit.

The rapid growth of students and faculty during the early fifties and the certain prospect of its acceleration in the years ahead demanded a more formal faculty structure with duties and procedures outlined in precise detail. The relaxed and genial informality in reaching decisions had to become precisely patterned. Department heads could no longer escape department meetings. It would no longer do to say to a major in the hall or after class, "So you had American Literature last semester, you must take Milton and the Novel next semester." As additional faculty members joined the department, courses could no longer be informally rotated. No longer could a faculty member teach a whole year as I did without having either an appointment or a contract from the Board of Trustees. Regulations as to discipline, the duties of committees, and housing had to be systematized. A certain amount of regimentation, however benign, was the cost of growth.

The first of these regulations outlined in detail the steps the Board established for appointment to the teaching staff. When a need in a department had been established, the department screened the list of candidates with great care before a recommendation was made to the Educational Policy Committee, which in turn interviewed the recommended candidates thoroughly and sometimes exhaustingly. If a colleague objected to the recommendation of the Educational Policy Committee, he had a right to present his case to the committee, and if unsatisfied with their further judgment, to the faculty, which could then sustain or reject his grievances. After passing all these tests, the candidate was interviewed by the Board, whose recommendation Synod almost invariably accepted. There were also rules concerning administrative offices other than that of the president.

I mention this in detail because President Spoelhof was always particularly concerned that the best available candidates be appointed. In this conviction the faculty joined him, and the quality of Calvin's faculty today is in large part a fruit of this idealistic and persistent effort on the part of all involved in the process of appointment.

By the early fifties Calvin's administrative officers were greatly overburdened. They had been overburdened for years, but by this time their duties had become herculean. A new administrative pattern emerged which was gradually refined during the years. New titles included Vice President for Academic Affairs; Dean of the College; Vice President for Business and Finance; Dean of Students; Director of the Library; College Chaplain; and Director of College . . . and Alumni Relations. Nine administrative positions were instituted. Today the administrative staff numbers forty. Fur-

thermore, college committees were reorganized and expanded and
their methods of operation carefully structured. These committees
now did a great deal of what had been formerly done in faculty
meetings, and thereby not only expedited the work of the faculty,
always in need of expedition, but also eliminated certain dramatic
interchanges characteristic of former faculty meetings. The rousing,
even eloquent, recommendations of candidates for scholarships began
to disappear as did the sometimes lengthy discussion of the merits
or demerits of preseminary students. This reorganization was accomplished without friction because of tactful and obviously necessary
recommendations of the president.

The steady growth of the college necessitating all these changes
began to crowd the college facilities intolerably. The additional buildings on the Calvin Campus included, as we have seen, the enlarged
Library (1950), the Science Building (1952), and the Commons
(1953). Even though these buildings were commodious and esthetically appealing, they proved inadequate, and the housing problem,
despite the purchase of attractive neighborhood homes, became vexing. Parking violations were proceeding at a steady clip of seventeen to twenty a week; the traffic officer patrolled his beat relentlessly,
and student fines led to chagrin and anger. Professors hurrying to
meet an eight o'clock class saw their spaces preempted. Some classes
met in the college and seminary chapels. Registration began in the
Science Building and was completed in the gymnasium, where students elbowed through narrow aisles and ended up more than once
to find their classes closed. The Library was often uncomfortably
filled with a slightly madding crowd; the generous library budget
jammed the stacks. Furthermore, the projected enrollment was expected to climb to 2,600 in fifteen years, which was, as it proved,
a very modest projection. The Board of Trustees, evaluating all these
facts, recommended to Synod in 1954 "that all construction save
emergency remodeling be halted pending a thorough study of needs."
A Long Range Planning Committee, appointed in 1949, was stream-
lined in 1955 and in great detail and in long meetings began considering the proper mode of physical expansion. In its desperate need for
facilities, it once considered plans to acquire the huge train shed
of the old Union Station for remodeling as a gymnasium. This plan
was dropped.

The first problem the Board faced was whether to expand its
facilities in the neighborhood or to abandon it. I use this rather
loaded word because it expresses the sentiments of those who felt

a loyalty to the life of the city and viewed leaving the area and
its looming tensions as a moral and spiritual retreat. These sentiments
were strongly expressed as the actual process of changing the campus
began, and strong pronouncements of spiritual defection appeared in
Chimes, sometimes by those who lived in suburban isolation themselves.

The Board and Synod approved the desire to move and then
faced three options: purchase of the 98-acre Ridgemoor Golf Course,
thoroughly familiar to many members of the faculty, purchase of the
150-acre Feenstra farm on East Burton, or purchase of the 166-acre
Knollcrest estate on Burton and the East Beltline, a baronial establishment on a harmoniously diversified landscape. In 1956, Synod
approved the purchase of the Knollcrest estate from Mr. J. C. Miller
for $400,000. Four years later, in 1960, the seminary was occupied
and largely paid for; in 1962 the Library Classroom building, containing thirteen classrooms and a most commodious library, was occupied. After the erection of many splendid buildings, the campus
was completely relocated.

The Knollcrest Barony at the time of purchase.

Knollcrest in 1962.

It was not easy for everyone to leave what Dean Rooks had called the "imposing edifice constructed of reinforced concrete and brick veneer." For thousands of alumni, Calvin connotes the imagery of pillared entrance to the Administration Building with its worn steps and the debris of smokers, the red Dormitory with the rustling tree at the door, the honed efficiency of the Science Building, the low porch and crowded doorways of the Commons, the quiet charm of the Hekman Library, and the dim and quiet chapel in the Hekman Memorial Seminary. The images may be colored by nostalgia, but there is still truth of impression in the very colorings. Here students hurried to classrooms to hear the professor or meet someone not in the books. In these classrooms and laboratories they learned gladly or sullenly, were bored or inspired, daydreamed or concentrated. In this chapel some were uplifted, some studied, and some slept. Inextricably woven into their memories are the lines and tones of these buildings, the geometrically severe classrooms, where the professor still stood on a podium. For many years they heard the peal of the chimes with its suggestion of other dimensions. No one can return to all these things, but few who have been there can erase them.

Idealism often costs much money and Calvin's new plans were going to demand staggering amounts of it. The money came from various sources, but genuinely impressive amounts came from the members of the Christian Reformed Church. In 1956 the Ford Foundation gave Calvin $100,000, and in addition, for its concern about faculty salaries, a bonus of $284,000, the interest of which was given to the faculty for many years. Eventually the principal was used to help finance the building program and faculty salaries were boosted more than commensurately. The "Needs of Today Campaign" operative for five years had raised over $1,300,000 since 1953 (January 1953 - December 1958). Though many feared that the spending was ill-considered, even reckless, contributions came grandly in. In 1958-59, the Calvin Envelope system was inaugurated, and these plus general solicitations raised almost $800,000 by 1962. The Campus Development Campaign from 1962 to 1966 raised a total of almost $1,900,000. The bulk of these gifts came from the loyal members of the denomination. Many men and women worked and gave sacrificially, but the college owes much to the financial acumen, great good sense, and cheery spirit of Henry De Wit, Vice-President of Financial Affairs, and Sidney Youngsma, whose verve, imagination, wit, and public relations savvy were invaluable to the college in his

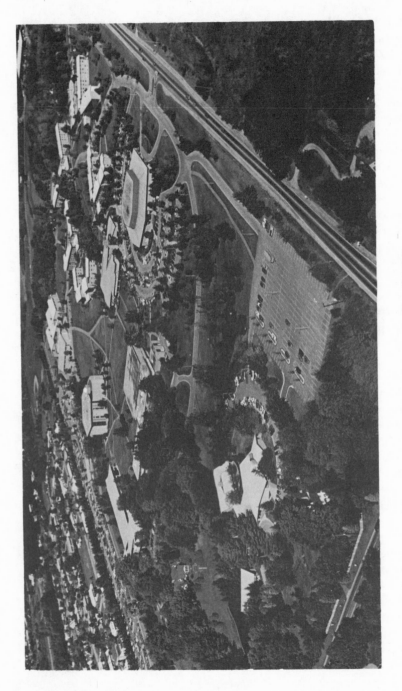

Knollcrest almost completed 1974.

work as Developmental Secretary. Very substantial grants and low-cost loans were also received from the government.

The Knollcrest campus, so called because Mr. Miller insisted that the name of the estate be retained, absorbed most of this money. The entire campus and its buildings were given a significant form, deliberately chosen to embody the ideals of its founders. President Spoelhof formulated these ideals, which after being adopted by the faculty with only slight modifications were given to the firm of Perkins and Will of Chicago for concrete embodiment.

These principles stressed the organic unity of all knowledge, to be expressed in the primacy of the "three most important facets of formal education represented by such buildings as classrooms and laboratories, chapel and library." The emphasis in placing the buildings should fall on the idea of a community of scholars. The Library-Classroom building, containing faculty offices as well, should exemplify the importance of the library in the constellation of buildings. The dormitories and Commons should effectively integrate student social life. Furthermore, there was a statement of the purposes each building served. Guided by these principles, the architects designed a campus delightful to the eye and congenially housing the activities of the college community.

From 1956, when Synod approved the purchase of Knollcrest, to 1973, when the college moved all its activities to the new campus, a great deal of administrative and faculty effort was absorbed by the bold new project. When the campus actually became split in 1963, many new problems of scheduling, housing, and transportation arose. All had to be dealt with, however difficult or tangled, while the regular work of the college proceeded. It was a time of hard work and at times of considerable inconveniences. Furthermore, always haunting the office of business affairs was the great difficulty of selling the old campus, a long, often frustrating affair.

The ordinary life of the college, which is, or should be, largely devoted to learning and thinking, is not impervious to the unexpected and stunning. This was true in the generally placid fifties and early sixties. Without any warning death struck with overwhelming immediacy. On September 28, 1961, Professor Henry R. Van Til of the Bible Department fell dead while talking to a friend in the Hekman Building. He was a man of apparently boundless vigor, rock-hard convictions, and unusual hospitality. He was outspoken, even militant, in his conviction, intolerant of what he considered erroneous ideas whether held by friend or foe. He had no use for compromise and could sometimes abrasively insist upon his point of view. He was unusually friendly and companionable, unaware that his zeal might disturb friendship. He had a deep love of preaching and was an eloquent preacher. He himself considered a preacher to be "not as soldiers on parade, but as on guard and in critical circumstances with readiness to fire." A volatile, colorful personality, his loss to the college, especially at such an early age, was indeed sad.

Dr. Cecil De Boer's sudden death five years earlier while trying to telephone friends he was ill was another stunning blow to the college community. His services to the college are remembered in another chapter in this book.

On December 2, 1956, at the age of forty-seven, Dr. Henry Zylstra died of a heart attack in Amsterdam, where he was teaching at the Free University on a Fulbright grant. His death caused poignant grief in the student body and faculty. Calvin lost an unusually gifted teacher, a distinguished scholar, a superb translator, an indefatigable writer on various levels of publication, and an acute educational counsellor. Fortunately many of his insights are available in the anthology *Testament of Vision,* gathered together by his friends. Dr. Zylstra was a superlative teacher. He had the indispensable undergirding of wide and meticulous scholarship and he illuminated it with an imaginative and spiritual reach that rose above the mediated detail to encounter the student with vision. He knew the authors he taught from the inside, what they meant for their age and for ours. His impressive knowledge of literature both traditional and contemporary and in various languages enabled him to put a sure finger on our current cultural agonies—what they mean and how we as Calvinists should assess them. This winnowing of values was done by an understanding heart which made the judgment humane and compelling. The sharing of learning was enhanced by a remarkably clear and resonant voice, sparkling phrases, sunny humor, and a rare dramatic gift. Even the fumbling in turning pages turned into suspense. He might ask a student a question and then answer it lengthily and eloquently himself. He might linger on a line to deliver a homily. His sense of humor ranged from devastating understatement to sidesplitting narrative. He understood the uncomfortable boy from the farm as well as his sophisticated classmate from the city. He gave something to the mediocre as well as the greatly talented. He never turned yellowing notes. He was a teacher, as one student put it, "whom the Christian community could not spare."

At Calvin College and in the community which supported it, he made an unusual impact on educational theory and practice. He was often sought as a speaker at teachers' conventions, where he spoke with uncommon charm and force. He was an original and creative member of the Educational Policy Committee. His aggressive idealism, high educational standards, and ceaseless efforts to improve both the understanding and character of Christian education left a permanent mark on Calvin College.

The death of Henry Zylstra marked also, as I see in retrospect, an end of an era in the college—the high point of professional impact and widespread institutional esteem. Never again was Calvin to see such mobilization of effort to honor the death and services of an esteemed colleague. A special, crowded memorial service in the Calvin Christian Reformed Church, splendid tributes in *Chimes,* the posthumous publication of a recording—such has not since happened. Only at the sad sudden death of Professor Rinck in 1920 and the departure of Dr. Jellema for Indiana University in 1935 had such high esteem been universally shown. At the death of Dr. John De Vries on November 23, 1967, another superlatively gifted teacher, nothing like it recurred.

The relatively small size of the faculty, the limited physical plant where high visibility was possible, the numerous clubs, sponsored by interested faculty members, the frequent repeated enrollment of a student in a professor's course—all contributed to widespread and often close acquaintance with members of the student body. I still remember that Faith Holtrop, now Mrs. Charles Orlebeke, was in so many of my classes that she seemed like a member of the family. As the college more than doubled in size, as the campuses were split, as the clubs disappeared, and the number of classes a professor taught decreased by a third, a professor's influence attenuated. It is in the classroom, club, and personal contact that a teacher's abiding influence is exerted. Whatever high achievement he produces in scholarly research, it is unlikely to be read by his students unless he makes them read his articles or buy his books. It is true, of course, that the overall excellence of the faculty was greatly increased in the sixties, but the profound personal impact diminished.

One has to read the old issues of *Chimes* and *Prism* to share the warm sun the older generation of professors luxuriously basked in, even though they may have been unaware of anything uncommon. When professors retired—often reluctantly—at seventy, they received a press inconceivable today. The professors themselves added to it; they had a real gift for intramural eulogy. Roger Heyns, as I noted, published an almost tearful editorial beseeching the Board to permit Dean Rooks to remain a few more years to stimulate the college by his very presence. The students gave banquets honoring retirees J. Broene and J. Nieuwdorp. In the late sixties professional influence was probably at its nadir. In late years student attitudes have again changed and without being maudlin, as they sometimes were, are realistically appreciative.

Retirement at Calvin, formerly mandatory at seventy, is now mandatory at sixty-five. I have heard most of the retirement speeches given at Calvin College, and to me they have been fascinating to hear. One knows the retiree is trapped before he begins to speak. He is, since without intelligence he would have never arrived at this spot, aware of the role he has to play and the self he would like to express. The role demands gratitude and grace; the self may well demand grudge and grimace. In some rare cases, I suppose, the role and the self may be identical, but I like to watch the wavering. The laconic farewell dodges the whole problem, the hortatory sermons mix the two, the lugubrious tirade certainly expresses the self. One can, of course, in all sincerity thank God for having been privileged to teach at Calvin with its thoroughly likeable students, its congenial colleagues, and an opportunity to teach in accordance with his deepest beliefs, but surely no intelligent man can be so unaware of irony, frustration, and defeat to honestly assess his teaching career at Calvin as I have heard it assessed by some. Surely, in this world even "in the greenest of green valleys/falls the appalling snow." If he is unaware of it, something will remind him of it. At one memorable occasion the special music consisted of a piece called "Here I Stand With One Foot in the Grave." The gentleman so honored still walks defiantly about in ironical comment.

The Calvin Pension Fund, formerly the main resource for the golden years, had been established in 1938 and supplemented by Social Security in 1951. It was altered in 1958, when the institution joined the Teachers Insurance and Annuity Association of America. This is an excellent plan, and the college, after a period of a fifty-percent contribution to the plan, now shoulders the entire cost as a fringe benefit. Calvin College has also been very generous in its insurance benefits.

In 1958 Calvin's educational opportunities were both assessed and fortified. A State Legislative Study Committee under the direction of Dr. John D. Russell published a study entitled "Instructional Programs in Michigan Institutions of Higher Education." This committee found little padding in Calvin's catalog; courses listed were not window-dressing but actually taught. Furthermore, the weighted average size of upper division classes at Calvin was 20.6 compared to 18.2 for all privately operated colleges in Michigan. The number of semester hours of different courses taught by the average faculty member at Calvin was 10.7, as compared with 7.7 at State colleges, but only one private college had a lower average than Calvin's. One private college had 24. Dr. Russell stated emphatically, however, that if high student-teacher loads were accompanied by excellent salaries and teachers, he had no criticism and he had none of Calvin. In 1958 Calvin applied for accreditation by the National Council for the Accreditation of Teacher Education. Preparation for this application involved an extended and arduous reorganization of the Teacher Education Program.

After a thorough examination for the North Central Association of Colleges, the North Central Review Team issued the following statement on November 17, 1961:

> Calvin College has developed an enviable reputation as a first-class liberal arts college, where students, faculty, and administration together reach a high level of academic achievement. The review team believes the record is deserved.

This reputation Calvin worked hard to maintain during the next decade by the appointment of carefully chosen and highly qualified teachers, by a massive reexamination and restructuring of the curriculum, and by greatly expanded facilities in which to do the work of the college.

A striking instance of Calvin's growing maturity and poise was revealed in its response during this decade to various plans in the denomination to establish junior colleges. Already in 1939 the Calvin Board had received a letter from five midwestern classes requesting aid in establishing a junior college, even though neither the debt of $10,000 which Western Christian High owed Calvin nor any of the interest on it for many years had been paid. It was never fully repaid, and by cancelling half the debt and all the interest Calvin made a substantial donation to Christian education in Iowa. The Board refused to accede to the new request because it felt such action would dissipate both the energy and money needed for Calvin's development. After World War II more pressure was applied, including such a request from Classis California. In 1948 the Board referred the problem to the Educational Policy Committee of the college. At a special meeting in 1950, the faculty advised strongly against such action; Synod concurred in this advice. When in 1952 the faculty was apprised that the establishment of a junior college in Sioux Center, Iowa, was planned, no attempt to discourage it was made, and a conference of administrators and other educators met at Calvin. Mutual steps in wise planning were undertaken, and President Spoelhof served the meeting and later the college with counsel. Dordt College in Sioux Center, Iowa, and Trinity College in Chicago have both developed into sound and promising institutions without imperilling Calvin's development. The older members of the faculty remember with real regret the fine students Calvin could not, as a consequence, enroll.

Nearly all was markedly different in Calvin's relationships with Grundy Seminary and College, established in 1916 to serve the German-speaking churches in Classis Oostfriesland and, as its first catalog states, "well located" in Grundy Center, Iowa, "a beautiful little 'city' of some 1600 inhabitants." Grundy Center, the catalog goes on to say, is "a 'clean' town and every effort will be put forth to protect our students." The school initially offered four years of high school, two of college, and three of seminary training. The Synod of the Christian Reformed Church, the Board of Trustees, and President Hiemenga were not greatly interested in protecting the institution. Grundy's initial prosperity was viewed jealously, its objectives were questioned, and Synod in 1918 ordered the termination of the Theological Department in 1920, though it graciously permitted the junior college to continue on the condition that it operate in the interests of pre-seminary students. Dr. George Stob in his book *The Christian Reformed Church and Her Schools* says:

> Professor D. H. Kromminga complained there were people who wanted to banish Grundy Center from the earth, and spoke of the "ill-will of the Curatorium and of those who have no love for Grundy Center."

I taught at Grundy Junior College as it was limping to demise, and I can testify to the lingering resentment against Calvin and even the church. One of my colleagues almost hated the church for its "betrayal" of Grundy College. Dr. Henry Beets, who did so much for Calvin, strongly supported Grundy College also. In the church itself Dr. Van Lonkhuyzen was not the only one who felt that Synod had acted like a Roman hierarchy. One can verify these feelings by checking the contributions to Calvin in *The Yearbook* of the Christian Reformed Church. In 1931, Classis Oostfriesland gave $611 to Calvin and $1263 to Grundy. Wellsburg I, its largest church, gave nothing to Calvin.

The long, crowded decade 1951-1962 had been an era of enthusiastic expansion and scarcely uninterrupted optimism. Enrollment had grown steadily from 1,470 in the fall of 1951 to 2,412 in the fall of 1961. The faculty had more than doubled and many first-class faculty members had been appointed. There had been strong student loyalty and notable civility. The key word of the era was probably *commitment*. There had been many strong calls in classrooms and publications for loyalty to Christ, His Word, and the Calvinistic heritage. Integration, it had been frequently emphasized, should not occur at the expense of the faith once delivered. The Student Council had a modest but real and growing influence. In 1959 the First Annual Fine Arts Festival was held. This event has become an important medium for artistic expression, display, and appreciation. Its yearly challenge to creative students has produced many commendable achievements in the fine arts. Relations between administration and faculty were highly cordial, and President Spoelhof had demonstrated his rare capacity for mediating disputes between the college and the constituency. Since he had the full respect of the faculty, he was able to lead effectively. The new campus, soon to be partially occupied, offered needed facilities and room. Calvin faced the dramatic sixties with an excellent administration, a highly competent faculty, a rarely gifted business manager and assistant, a concerned Board, and an overwhelmingly loyal constituency. It would need them all. It would need to be strengthened by three elements of the Calvin community, which will be briefly described before we look at the long years of stress, strain, and successful adjustment.

CHAPTER SEVEN

TWO CORNERSTONES AND A SHELTERING TREE

—1—
IN A COLLEGE CHAPEL

In a College Chapel is the title of a book by Professor J. Broene published in 1928. In addition to miscellaneous addresses, the volume contains a number of chapel talks which served as models for excellent chapel talks in his era, or any era as far as I can see. These talks with their calm wisdom, dignity, and poise reveal an effectively interwoven pattern of learning and spiritual insight, expressed in a restrained and polished style. They range from terse psychographs of such Biblical characters as Jacob, Rehoboam, and Peter to an analysis of the relations of a student to his culture in "Worldliness" and "The Wages of Sin." There are notably illuminating talks on the professions. The volume is long out of print, but its charm and insight make it worth reading today.

Chapel services at Calvin have been one of the most analyzed, debated, criticized, occasionally praised, and, in the last years, most experimental features of life at Calvin College. Students have come sluggishly or eagerly, perforce or voluntarily, for spiritual ends or "You'd better see him about it at chapel." While there, students have listened, slept, studied, or daydreamed. Some have wanted meaty discussions about religion and culture, some pep talks, some amusement. Some have argued that chapel would provide a good opportunity for Glee Clubs to "practice up." Some have said students ought to be charitable to the drafted professors for giving talks since "they are not being paid for that." There has been vigorous skipping, and professors have been asked to prowl the halls and restrooms to constrain students to come in. Their attendance has been checked and photographed, but some outwitted surveillance and cheated on attending. One student won an intercollegiate prize in journalism by describing the ways in which some beat the system. These attitudes and activities impelled a sizable consumption of print.

126

A little book could be compiled solely devoted to student re-action to chapel. Editorials in *Chimes,* as well as letters to the editor, have grumbled, praised, and endlessly advised. Chapel talks have been described as mechanical, lifeless, irrelevant, and unfit for a sophisticated college student. The variety of student behavior and attitude is reflected in these lines from the *Prism* of 1959:

> *"Take my life and let it beeeee—"*
> *(Filled with facts for my history bluebook).*
> *The song is over. Students settle down*
> *To think, sleep, whisper, worship.*
> *Often a speech will redirect the way to God.*
> *Often, it rehashes themes too familiar to reach*
> *Sophisticated college students.*

It is small wonder that faculty members often found conducting chapel one of the hardest duties they had to perform.

During the sixties the criticisms became sharper. Outside speakers were increasingly used, diversified programs introduced, the faculty largely eliminated. Little groups of students organized to meet pe-culiar needs. Chapel became largely voluntary; then wholly voluntary. The argument that voluntary chapel would stimulate attendance was proved the myth it always was. Student criticism died out. The vocal critics were now attending to their own spiritual needs. Novel spir-itual menus were introduced, but it is perfectly clear that the only way to insure universal attendance of faculty and students is by compulsion, and that today is neither desirable nor possible.

Already in 1900 chapel was compulsory. It was scheduled at 7:45 A.M.; the temptation to skip was hard to resist and many stu-dents overcame it, as Oscar Wilde says, by yielding to it. Already in these early years all the old chestnuts were hurled at chapel; vol-untary chapel would insure attendance, erase hypocrisy, create bet-ter attitudes. Compulsory chapel was, however, maintained, and in the September 2, 1911, issue of *The Grand Rapids Press,* the writer says that Calvin "challenges any college in the country to produce a better percentage of chapel attendance." The college insured this reputation by maintaining compulsory chapel until 1925.

Students are not known as gentle critics; and, unfortunately, most of the printed assessments of chapel services are somewhat stri-dent, and, I believe, unrepresentative. There is, of course, no way of proving this judgment. My own recollections of chapel services at Calvin include memories of mechanical services, conducted with minimal preparation and effort, but much more numerous memories of carefully produced, imaginative, and moving talks, lively and relevant to the needs of the students and the context of the occasion. I regret the contemporary exclusion of most of the faculty from the services; I miss the spiritual stimulation many gave through insight, devotion, and style.

In addition to recurrent pleas for a voluntary chapel, the students sought a college pastor. Already in *Chimes* in 1917, J. Van Beek has a solidly reasoned, four-page editorial arguing its necessity. Van Beek maintains that the growing size of the school makes close personal contact between professors and students difficult. A college pastor would have an open office and an open heart for them all. He would associate intimately with the dormitorians and thereby exercise a refining influence upon them. The chaplain should be a "thoro American," a "good mixer," possessing an "anti-colonial spirit," a scholar "able to give courses in theology," and a profoundly Christian gentleman. Van Beek urges the student body to petition the Board for such an appointment. He urges also that the student body guarantee half his salary. In 1921 *Chimes* again pleads for such a pastor:

> Is it not apparent that our school is in need of a college pastor . . . who can be a true spiritual father to us, helping solve our problems and overcome our perplexing difficulties?

The plea is strongly reiterated in 1925. This article suspects stiff opposition in high places, but adds that "repeated blows will break the stone." There are other similar pleas and common to them all is the emphasis on the pastoral aspect of the position, the personal interest and concern students hope to acquire. They want someone to talk to. The request was partially fulfilled by the appointment of Dr. Henry Meeter as Professor of Bible, but he was immediately so overwhelmed with course work that personal contact became fractional. It was not until 1962 that the appointment of Reverend Mr. Bernard Pekelder satisfied the need for a full-time chaplain, an office he has filled with distinction.

In 1925 voluntary chapel was temporarily introduced. The faculty set no shining example of attendance; neither did they exercise a masterfully persuasive influence upon the students, "some being very strict while others allowed considerable latitude," as the faculty minutes of April 13, 1927, report. On March 9, 1928, the matter was still vexing the faculty, and the faculty decided that since some students were lolling about in various parts of the building instead of going to chapel, "two members of the Faculty [should] pass through the building in the course of chapel exercises to determine who are guilty of this infraction of rules and report such." So some of the faculty went silently gliding about; but these private eyes were ineffective also. Yet, the faculty did not return to forced attendance, and, despite some regular absentees, chapel attendance was generally good, though never good enough. When the veterans returned, the problem grew, and on April 22, 1947, the Committee on Religious Activity reported "that it will support the President in whatever measures he may deem it necessary to take in regard to chapel attendance." Administrative control of chapel included various compulsory measures from checking to photography, from exhortation to discipline, until 1971, when the faculty temporarily adopted a system of chapel "without the regulations regarding attendance." At first students and faculty could sign a pledge to attend if they so wished. At present there is no pledge; and all chapel attendance is voluntary twice a week.

At the beginning of his work in 1962, Rev. Pekelder submitted an interesting and stimulating paper to the Chapel Committee in which he defines the place of chapel in the college community. He points out that no person can be neatly divided into "a learning and a believing entity": he is always both and remains such even in a distinct way of life. Since college deals with the total person, it inescapably deals with his spiritual life and does so at all times. As a religious person, the student participates in the "communion of saints," and chapel exists to minister to this communion. It does so not through academic lectures, or abbreviated church services, nor through diversion, but as a manifestation of "complete worship for students and faculty where the peculiar needs of the college community are served." Chapel exists to enrich the spiritual life of the college through essentially devotional worship. The college chapel should be a "focal point of religious expression for the college community."

The final decontrolling of chapel in 1971 was not done lightly. A long and, whatever its weaknesses, fruitful tradition was to be scrapped; not, of course, the idea of the value of chapel as an important aspect of student life, but the idea that it was so important an aspect of student life that students should not be allowed to neglect it. The clamorous criticism of required chapel, the powerful dimensions of student opinion in the last years, and a faculty reassessment of the idea of compulsory chapel brought about the change. In 1967 a student survey indicated that only eighteen percent of the student body approved compulsory chapel, that forty-two percent gave it a qualified approval, and that thirty-eight percent disapproved entirely. Only thirty-four percent of the student body pledged that they would attend chapel voluntarily. In the face of such sentiments and the virtual impossibility of dignified and adequate monitoring of chapel sessions, compulsory chapel was abandoned. Furthermore, the nature of the chapel service was greatly modified. Vocal students consistently complained that chapel services had a kind of metronomic monotony, that they are "dull, trite, boring, uninspired." An exegetically sound message tailored to making students "capable of living the Christian life in contemporary society" was no longer enough. Consequently, the structure of chapel services has been greatly altered. The faculty debated the matter at length and most seriously and finally consented to a trial period of voluntary chapel.

In the fall of 1974, Calvin had four chapel services a week in the Fine Arts Center, two of which were repeats. The attendance at all four services was about 1500-2000 a week, depending on the appeal of the previously announced service. The enrollment at Calvin in the fall of 1974 was 3,414 students. The faculty numbered 159. The informal fellowship services attract about a hundred students a week, and the foreign-language services about the same. There is no way of determining how many students seldom or never attend chapel, but it is a sizable number. Nor have all faculty members consistently attended. Whether out of conviction, inertia, indifference, other business, or amplitude of spiritual resources, many are seldom there.

Chapel services today are markedly varied. In addition to conventional chapel talks, other media have been introduced to interest and challenge students. Programs consist of contemporary music, often folk music with guitars, groups of singers from quartets to the Cappella Choir, illuminated paintings interwoven with the appropriate readings from Scripture, brief plays or films, hymn sings, and creative dance. Furthermore, in the smaller chapels one can worship in German, Dutch, French, or Spanish. The Fellowship Chapel utilizes informal procedures in singing, speaking, and posture. "Let everything that hath breath praise the Lord!"

Since chapel is now voluntary, criticism of it has all but ceased. The spirit of those that attend is spiritual and markedly receptive. Failure to support chapel services in the past was never wholly a matter of dissatisfaction with the services themselves. Intelligent and spiritual members both of the student body and faculty have never been convinced that chapel is a necessary element in a Christian college whose classrooms professedly embody a religious spirit. Whether this is so or not, chapel to me at least has always seemed a rewarding exercise of Christian fellowship and worship in a devotional dimension unfeasible in the classroom. I am certain that many alumni cherish moments in the chapel services which moved them personally in long-lasting ways. There were also moments of moving unity in certain memorial services for students and faculty suddenly wrenched from life. Emily Dickinson once said:

> *A word is dead*
> *When it is said,*
> *Some say.*
> *I say it just*
> *Begins to live*
> *That day.*

Many who attended chapel services at Calvin will remember words, here and there, that lodged firmly and bore much fruit.

—2—
IN A COLLEGE LIBRARY

"A book," says I. A. Richards, in a definition reflecting his naturalistic psychology, "is a machine to think with." Milton, at the other pole of imagery, calls a great book "The precious life blood of a master spirit." Thoreau says, "A written word is the choicest of relics." The Word of the Lord was written in "the roll of a book" (Jeremiah 36:2). The character of a college library goes a long way toward defining the quality of a college. A college library need not and ordinarily cannot abound in first or rare editions, but if it is to serve the college well, it must house the volumes and magazines necessary to a successful pursuit of its academic ideals. Some students, indeed, enter the library only under compulsion and while there chat and chew and leaf through magazines; not all professors go home laden with books; but even if underused or misused, the library is at the heart of a college. It takes years to build a reputable library and a great amount of money. No library ever really arrives, and the increasing cost of books and publications today threatens the quality of many college libraries. A brief word should be devoted to the history of Calvin's library; into it went much money, much shrewd planning, and a great deal of intelligent concern.

The library in the early "school of the parsonage" comprised the books of the minister who taught the school. The Theological School and the Preparatory Department did not have a library room until the school moved to Franklin and Madison in 1892. During these early years many prospective ministers like my father spent every available cent they had for theological works in order to provide valuable resources for use in the culturally isolated communities they might be called to serve. The nature of the early library, I have been unable to discover, but it is safe to speculate that many of its books were derived from the studies of the clergy. The first gift toward books was made by Mrs. E. Vanden Berge in 1896. This gift was to serve as the basis of a permanent library fund. In 1900 an official register of purchased books was begun. It consists of page after page, with fifty entries to a page, all written in a most elegant script. By 1911 the library consisted of 4,000 volumes. A feature article in *The Grand Rapids Press,* September 2, 1908, states that "the library is suffering from the lack of proper accommodation; and the need of better reading room facilities is urgent." The *Chimes,* in retrospect, says in 1917, "Deplorable indeed was the condition of the library department in the old building. The room was cramped even with the relatively few volumes." It was not until 1928 that the need for better quarters was filled. During the years 1900-1918, 5,051 volumes, largely dealing with theology and the humanities, were purchased. It is interesting to observe that many of the volumes were purchased through moneys given by people unconnected with the church. The register from 1918 to 1921 is unavailable. In 1915 budget allowances for the various departments had to be "systematized," a euphemism for *controlled.* Some departments were preempting the treasury.

The second extant register covers the years 1921-1928, at the end of which period the number of volumes had reached 16,750. Interest in a good library was shared by the students, who rejoiced at the new facilities, meagre as they really were, at the Administration Building in 1917. Here, for the first time, a card system was introduced, and it was announced that "the library would be open a few hours each day." The "splendid reading room" was made available during these few hours. One is struck by this gratitude when remembering the nonchalance with which the truly splendid appointments of the present Library-Classroom Building were greeted by many students. In the *Chimes* of May 1918, Associate Editor R.

Stob notes that "our library has improved wonderfully during the past two or three years." Stob also notes that the library has particularly improved in making available books that create a "friction of ideas"; each book "sharpens the insight into truth." The library, Stob concludes, is less parochial; philosophical and literary works are being added, scientific volumes, critical works on Scripture—all enabling the student to develop a broader application of the Calvinistic perspective.

In 1925, Professor R. Stob wrote an interesting article for *The Banner* entitled "The Library of Calvin College." He makes a strong plea for a library representing Athens as well as Jerusalem. He admits that the library "during the first years was but a rather insignificant part of the institution." He adds that "since about 1915 the increase has been considerable." In 1925 the library consisted of 12,000 volumes, and the volumes chosen were generally admirable. As evidence, he adds that "We are far on the way to having a complete collection of the works of Kuyper and Bavinck." The basis for forming a genuinely Reformed perspective, says Stob, is available. If someone should ask, "Is there no end to the purchase of books, are we not ever to be satisfied?", the answer is no. A good library can only grow, and Calvin's Library did. The third register includes the years 1928-1944, and the holdings at the end of the period stood at 28,500. By 1947 the total was 32,000. After this date, the holdings grew dramatically. During the Spoelhof administration the volumes including periodicals and their indices grew to over 250,000. In the school year 1973-1974, 10,815 volumes were added. The zeal of the administration, faculty, and librarians Josephine Baker, Lester De Koster, and Marvin Monsma for a fine library has been generously supported by the Board. The present library with its books, appointments, and genially excellent librarians is a proper source of pride and deep gratitude to God. In addition to constantly growing accessions, three major events should be noted in establishing the library of Calvin College.

"Thursday, March 8 [1928] marked a red letter day in the history of Calvin College and Theological School," according to an editorial in *The Banner* by Dr. H. Beets. He describes with obvious enthusiasm the dedication of the Hekman Memorial Library, given to the school by Mrs. E. Hekman, Sr., and her children. At this occasion the college auditorium was crowded, and the audience listened with "rapt attention" to speeches by S. H. Ranck, librarian of the Grand Rapids Public Library, and Professor L. Berkhof of

Calvin Seminary, as well as to two shorter speeches and two "musical numbers." Mr. Ranck emphasized the role a library performs in fashioning the character as well as the mind of a student. Professor Berkhof stressed the fact that the library is an expression of faith in God's blessing upon a threefold task: to build a strong small college in an age which regards such colleges as passé; to strengthen a denominational college in an age which regards them as divisive; and to equip the library to provide a permanent memorial to Calvinism and its development in our culture. The audience responded enthusiastically not only to these speeches but also to the remainder of the program, after which they enjoyed the functional beauty of the building itself.

The new library was exciting and marvellously welcome. Gone was the stuffy little corner in the basement of the Administration Building, where you saw only the books the attendants brought you. Gone was the constriction. Here was a building ample in space, admirably convenient, and pleasantly equipped. It was a very attractive building in line and color; it suggested retreat without isolation, enjoyment as well as spartan scholarship. No student today can really appreciate the delight of the comfortable chairs in which to peruse the immediately available magazines and newspapers, the instantly available reference works and the inviting furniture on which to use them. For the 320 students of Calvin in 1928, it was a luxurious place. Though the time was years before the day of open stacks and semi-private study quarters, the change was dramatic to us, and every student who cared about books silently echoed the felicitous public expressions of gratitude expressed to the Hekman family for this fine gift. It is, furthermore, a happy thought to know that the Grand Rapids School of Bible and Music, which now owns the building, regards it with affection and maintains it with scrupulous care.

The serenity of the building was not always respected. Once a student lit a giant firecracker which shattered both nerves and lights. Once a student playing baseball in the field between the Dormitory and the library drove a hard liner through the window, past the librarian, who made no attempt to field it, after which it bounced to the other wall. After the players moved to the longer field between the Dormitory and Benjamin Avenue, several hard liners went through the windows on Benjamin, and Janitor Norden was in a rage and President Kuiper abolished campus baseball. Students have also stolen and defaced books. One student ripped out the section on Poe in the encyclopedia. Theological books have also disappeared.

In the late sixties the basement rooms were rented to a very progressive school, whose very progressive pupils made a mess of their quarters. The changing neighborhood also produced vandalism to the building and even danger to students who worked there until late hours.

The leap in enrollment in the fall of 1946 reduced the library from amplitude to insufficiency in three months' time. What had been luxury for 503 students in June became congestion for 1,245 students in September. The building became nerve-wrackingly cramped. Book shelves spilled into aisles; the 140 chairs in the reading rooms were wholly occupied, and students were driven to study outdoors in fair weather and to various unlikely places indoors about the campus in foul. Books were scarce; in some classes where two books had been adequate for outside reading, ten were needed now. Calvin's 32,000 volumes were suddenly meagre. The library was understaffed; there was no time to acquire proper help. Miss Baker did noble work but needed specialized help, not instantly available. The need was pressing, and after four hectic years was largely met by the addition of a splendid new wing in 1950, the greatly accelerated purchasing of books, and the addition of qualified assistants and librarians.

At the dedication of the new wing on June 30, 1950, Dr. Henry Zylstra delivered an address with the altogether characteristic title "The Indefeasible Title of Conquest." He began by saying, "We celebrate today a growth in depth." In former days at Calvin, when books were scarce, most learning came through text, lecture, and recitation. As a library grows, learning through research is increasingly necessary and possible. The speech focussed on creative scholarship, on a solid development of Reformed perspectives on learning. Zylstra said, "We have no university to appeal to, and must be our own university, irrespective of what degrees we may offer." We must be thoroughly knowledgeable about our own tradition to counter opposing philosophies. The true scholar needs the Book and books. The new facilities and the prospects of greatly increased holdings make possible the kind of spiritual conquest Calvin is concerned about.

The spiritual conquest Dr. Zylstra recommended required a constant strengthening of the resources of the library from encyclopedias and reference works to current magazines and bound copies of influential magazines. It would also demand as complete a collection as possible of the works of Calvin and the works on Calvinism in

printed volumes or on microfilm. There would also have to be built
a treasury of our own past to stimulate an awareness of our roots
in this country. Simultaneously, the volumes essential to scholarly
work in the subjects taught at Calvin would have to be steadily
enriched. All these matters have been attended to with great care
and at great cost.

The new wing added in 1950 provided only temporary relief.
As the college enrollment increased year after year, the library again
became overcrowded in every respect. By the fall of 1962, the enrollment was 2,537, and the new Library-Classroom Building was
occupied with gratitude. For eight years there were two Calvin
libraries, one at Knollcrest and one at the Hekman Memorial Library.
Finally, in 1970, the entire library was housed in the spacious, beautiful, and highly functional new library, a modular structure, since
the classrooms in the building could be converted into library rooms
when necessary.

In the summer of 1970 the completed library was dedicated,
and Dr. Lester De Koster, whose labors as librarian revealed great
vision and skill, delivered an address, "Philobiblon," of the love of
books. He spoke in the long shadows of the Vietnam War, the stri-
dent voices of student unrest and social upheaval. He finds on the
campus, "Where the true Rock is known, honored, adored, and truly
served," a place of hope. Here, aided by the superb resources of the
library, the Word of God can be proclaimed and strength acquired.
Here "we dedicate a noble building and fine collection, a library
well rounded and rich in holdings, for service to God and man."

This "noble building and fine collection," containing 250,000
volumes of books and bound periodicals is conveniently located for
both college and seminary. Current periodicals number 1,750; the
Library of American Civilization and the Library of English Literature are available in microfilm. The entire collection of microfilm,
microfiche, and microcards numbers 17,000. Individual study carrels,
lounge seating, and seminar rooms provide comfortable accommodation for 1,100 persons. Special collections are found in the Curriculum Center, the H. H. Meeter Calvinism Research Collection,
which is one of the most extensive repositories of books on Calvin
and Calvinism in the world, and the Cayvan Room, enriched by
the generosity of Mr. Llewellyn L. Cayvan, containing many records
and tapes for the study and enjoyment of music, speech, and literature. The Calvin Library also houses 28,000 items of government
documents.

The lower level of Heritage Hall is devoted to the story of our own past not only in books, magazines, pamphlets, but in a great variety of raw materials for new stories, histories, and reassessments. This fascinating collection owes its origin to a Synodical decision in 1934. In that year the Denominational Historical Committee was mandated to collect all available documents, records, reports, and other suitable memorabilia concerning the history of the Christian Reformed Church and to store them in a conveniently located site. After a modest beginning with the materials accumulated by Henry Beets and D. H. Kromminga and a modest showcase for notable items, more energetic efforts along articulate guidelines were initiated in 1951. In 1968, even more formal guidelines were adopted. Dr. De Koster, the archivist, was to superintend the storing of materials, and the immensely valuable services of Mr. E. R. Post were obtained as field agent. Originally designated as the Colonial Origins Collection, the materials are now known as the Heritage Hall Historical Collection, since the materials there found go far beyond those emerging from the Kolonie. Synod designated as belonging to these archives all the minutes of Synod and its official agencies.

The materials assembled in Heritage Hall are numerous, diverse, and often fascinating as well as illuminating. Personal papers, usually in the original, burst from certain boxes, so that one wonders if the author ever tore up a letter. There are many manuscripts, once rousing speeches, treasured a lifetime and now forgotten, reports, sermons, and memoirs. Books and magazine articles by and about members of the church line the walls. Our *literary* output may not have been enormous but we surely have written! Consistorial and classical minutes are neatly arranged in row upon row of microfilms, protected from badly motivated prowlers by the necessity of written permission from the organizations involved before any examination occurs. Anniversary booklets and pictures of churches are being collected. Anything of interest is being sought unless too large to store. There is room for the large brass key of the old Spring Street Church, but hardly room for church bells or old pulpit furniture. People of prominence in the history of the church are being immortalized in a biographical file replete with photographs and clippings. The industry and skill of the collectors is everywhere present.

The Heritage Hall Historical Collection should never be a dead letter office, where we systematically store the hopes, fears, frustrations, plots, jealousies, and abiding faith of other generations in an elegant grave. Whether one picks up a broadside advertising the sale of four oxen for eighty dollars, or follows the wavering morality in an old dispute, or hears a German pastor complaining that Synod in 1902 takes a pleasure cruise on Lake Michigan without deigning to consider his offer to translate the Dutch Church Order for the German churches, one finds the throb of humanity. The past is, I suppose, never wholly recoverable, but it sweeps over you movingly in this place.

—3—

THE ALUMNI OF CALVIN COLLEGE

Alma Mater is but one of the many old Latin phrases describing college life. If one attends college a year, no matter what one has done there, one becomes an alumnus, alumnae, or more diplomatically and grotesquely, an "alumperson." Once you have an alma mater, you are never forgotten; her concern and love pursue you from address to address, year after year, until you rest where the mailman never knocks. She regards her children with love in one eye and expectation in the other. She lets you in on all the news and how to pay for it. The year or more spent with the nourishing mother requires a lifetime to repay. It is easy to misinterpret this solicitude and to view her intentions with cynicism, but they are not dishonorable and in the college itself genuine affection for and pride in the alumni are not rare.

Such affection and pride begin while the alumni are still prospective. I doubt whether any teacher at Calvin has been unaware of the congenial and select character of the student body. Most of Calvin's teachers have taught at other schools before coming to Calvin, and they have all studied at them. I think all would say that Calvin students compare favorably with those of the vast majority of American colleges. The student body may not be thick with geniuses, but neither is it dense with dullards. Some come unprepared. The ignorance I have seen is more than mere ignorance; it is more than mere talent—it approaches genius. Some have survived intact all attacks by grammarians. When a professor, forced to use two editions of a text, said, "They are exactly alike except for the pagination," a student raised his hand and said, "But the pages are numbered different too." Some, indeed, come "to play sports," and some to waste an hour well. These are a decided minority. The intelligence of the student body is clearly above average, and in religious commitment, moral stance, and innate courtesy, it has clearly been exceptional. Many students, as their careers show, have been highly gifted. All of us can, I think, remember little acts of kindness. I could fill a page with them . . . from the four boys who literally lifted my car out of a rut on a cold winter day to the boy who came and washed and waxed the floor while my wife was ill. The faculty can thank God for the general character of the student body. There have been few highly developed sinners.

Some students are remembered if not for their acts and classroom performances, then for the unforgettable insights they have shared on their examination papers. To my surprise I learned, for example, that "Herbert George Wells, an English navelist [sic] was formerly on the staff of Calvin College," and that "Thomas Aquinas, a Lutheran, was the author of *The Doomsday Book,* converting the people through the nation." A few years before, "Harold Agrippa had nipped the early church in the but." Poe, the author of "The House of the Fallen Ushers," was a "very emotional man, all the women he loved died." Irving "used native familiarities in presenting Ichabod Crane, who was very loose." A *shroud* is a "small animal, clever, sneaky," a *blight* is "something frivolous," a *swain* is "an animal like a pig" or "waterfowl, filthy." I have been told that "when two people get married they become part of an heroic couplet who have a hard time together." In telling me why they came to Calvin, freshmen have given the following reasons: "to keep the standard of living high," "to keep the human race going up hill," and "to get a basically good underground for the future life." The latter is important information because, as a student wrote, "We are all part of the dead and should face death confidentially." Whether brilliant, bright, ordinary, or a little under, the students have been a source of pride and pleasure. One of the tests of Calvin's academic integrity as shrinking enrollments appear imminent will be its determination not to accommodate itself to illiteracy and mediocrity.

The alumni of Calvin have from her early years enhanced her reputation. Already in 1913, G. Keizer writes from Ann Arbor in an Alumni Letter to *Chimes:*

> Before closing let me say that there is something upon which Calvin students are to be congratulated. I refer to the fact that Calvin College stands so high in scholarship with the university authorities. Calvin graduates are accepted without question. Such matters serve to make me only the more proud of our Alma Mater.

In 1920 a medical student writes about his application to Rush Medical School, "I was gratified to find that I was immediately accepted. Calvin College had such a high reputation that other top grad schools were glad to get its graduates." The students who have pursued graduate work all the years to the present have maintained this reputation; many such students have returned to Calvin to teach. In 1953, Robert H. Knapp and Joseph J. Greenbaum, in *The Younger American Scholar; His Collegiate Origins,* report that in the years 1946-1951 Calvin College ranked forty-fifth in the nation in terms of "the highest percentage of graduates who are awarded Ph.D.'s or University fellowships." There is no reason to believe the percentage has dropped.

The Alumni of Calvin have brought honor to the college in many ways. To list even a fraction of these achievements would consume pages; to list the important but unpublicized contributions of her graduates to church, school, and community would fill the book. From the first appearance of "Calvinalia" in *The Banner* to the latest issue of *The Calvin Spark,* many of these achievements have been recorded. They constitute a striking evidence of God's grace to a small, struggling group of immigrants. Calvin has been permitted to help some of them and many of their descendants move from rags to riches, from social scorn through sanction to success, from vulnerability to comfort. Above all it has developed in its graduates a greater sense of the presence in and responsibility for the Kingdom of God. None would claim that either Calvin or her alumni has fulfilled the ideal asserted by Professor Berkhof in 1926 when he gave the reason for Calvin's existence. Calvin, he says,

> finds its reason for existence in the Reformed principles for which we stand. The great task to which it is expected to address itself, is to apply these principles in every field of study, as the nature of the case may demand, and to exhibit their bearing on life in all its phases.

Calvin is still struggling with this problem. The Board-faculty conference in February 1975 discussed it energetically. A similar goal had but recently been reasserted in *Christian Liberal Arts Education,* which states that the goal of the college is

> to train the student to become a leader or perceptive follower in the tasks of molding society according to Christian standards and promoting Christian culture.

Whereas the former quotation is a permanent challenge to the staff, the latter implies as hard a task for the graduate—an almost immeasurably complex task in our fragmented culture, where anyone who wishes to make either a witness or an impact needs moral nerve and stamina, vision and grace.

Many of Calvin's alumni have responded to the college with interest, affection, and loyalty. In the early years of the school, R. Stob, Associate Editor of *Chimes,* made a plea to the alumni in the somewhat archaic rhetoric of the day:

> Oh, we graduates, more practical love for our institution. What a stimulus that would be to laymen in the church to do more also. The glory of us as an institution and as a church will be greatly enhanced.

Even prior to that, *Chimes* in 1911 suggests a way the alumni can garner support for the college. It proposes that alumni persuade the Mannen Vereenigingen (Men's Societies) in the denomination to contribute ten cents per member toward Calvin. This, *Chimes* says, would be a most effective medium since these societies "usually represent the best element in our churches." But the best way to show interest in the school proved to be the formation of an Alumni Association. The early history of the Alumni Association is largely lost or misplaced. Not until the meeting of the Board in 1930 are there available records. However, there are scattered sources here and there. According to Dr. H. Beets, president of the Alumni Association in 1920, Dr. W. Bode, later president of Grundy Seminary, first "agitated the matter" of an alumni association, and the first Calvin Alumni Association was organized on April 9, 1907. It had already been suggested in a meeting on March 21, where the Reverend Mr. J. Bolt of Cleveland had pointed out the importance of such an association. The Association cancelled its first public meeting for a lack of speeches, a want seldom experienced again. On September 4, 1907, the fall meeting was well attended with a highly literary menu of four orations. A second public meeting was held on June 11, 1908. Attended by a "host of friends" from various states, it appears to have been very successful with five orations. From 1908 to 1920, even with the abundance of orators or possibly because of them, the meetings were thinly attended for years. In 1920, Dr. Beets scolds and exhorts his fellow alumni for their inertia. "It is hard," he fumes, "to enthuse the ordinary Dutchman for something new." The Alumni Association had been dozing along for thirteen

years. He then complains that the graduates of Calvin "in a rep-
rehensible way fail to show the proper kind of interest," and
pleads, "Let us swell the ranks, fill the exchequer, put 'pep' in the
association."

His pleas were heard, and in 1920 the matter was "agitated
again" by a small group including Dr. G. Broodman, Helen Zandstra,
and Henry Ryskamp. They arranged what proved to be a highly
successful Association meeting during the Christmas vacation of
1920. In October 1925 the first alumni letter appeared. The letter
appeared regularly until the arrival of *The Calvin Spark* in 1953,
which has been published by the Calvin Alumni Association ever
since.

One of the interesting features of *Chimes* up to the fifties was
the regular inclusion of letters from Alumni, regularly solicited and
placed by an Alumni editor for a specific alumni department. The
letters came from near (Ann Arbor) and far (Africa). They range
from newsy chit-chat to ponderous exhortation, from wit and humor
to edged comments by the allegedly and newly emancipated. Gradually these letters faded away as the growing size of graduating classes
dissipated both their interest and that of the remaining students.
Increasing size whether in the classroom or the entire college, though
in many ways welcome, has many built-in disadvantages. It is always
interesting to watch an institution proudly advertising the advantages
of a small college, seeking to increase its enrollment.

In the early thirties Professor E. Y. Monsma, always genially
concerned about both students and alumni, became one of the prime
movers of the activities of the Association. The Calvin Alumni Association sponsored chapters throughout the country and abroad.
Today there are twenty-three chapters, radiating from Grand Rapids,
which has no chapter, to Hawaii, the Netherlands, and Alaska. The
director's report consumes thirteen pages. In July 1965, Mr. James
P. Hoekenga became the first full-time director of alumni affairs,
a post he has filled with unusual distinction. The Calvin Alumni
Association is governed by a board of fifteen members, who serve for
three years and are elected by ballot from all alumni. The Association annually awards two Distinguished Service Awards to nationally
recognized alumni and two Outstanding Service Awards to alumni
and non-alumni who have contributed singularly impressive services
to Calvin College.

The Calvin Alumni Participation Fund, composed of gifts by
alumni, finances many worthwhile activities including the ever wel-

come appearance of *Spark* four times a year, an alumni directory
with over 22,000 entries, a desk-pad calendar, a freshman grant
program, and upper classmen scholarships. It furnishes an extensive
repertoire of varied faculty speakers and encourages the individual
chapter in various ways. The multifarious activities of Homecoming
are carefully arranged each year through its office.

The alumni of Calvin College have given impressive support
to the college. Thousands of them contribute directly and liberally to
the Alumni Association. Since most of them belong to the Christian
Reformed Church, they contribute steadily to the Synodical quota
for Calvin. Furthermore, many have contributed to drives for funds
as well as employing their energies in soliciting them. It is, according to Mr. Hoekenga, safe to assume that over eighty percent of Calvin's alumni contribute to the support of the college. I doubt whether
any American college can improve on that record. As the diverse
strains on private institutions mount, the loyalty of Calvin's alumni
is crucially important. As a source of prospective students, intellectual
encouragement, loyal community support, and spiritual concern,
Calvin's alumni are indispensable to her Reformed development and
integrity.

CHAPTER EIGHT

LATITUDES UNKNOWN

In the fall of 1962, Calvin began its ten-year shift to the Knoll-crest campus. Freshmen classes were held in the Library-Classroom Building, and the dining hall as well as several residence halls were used. In 1966 the sophomore class was moved to Knollcrest. Year after year students and faculty were leaving familiar streets with their rich connotations. Franklin and Benjamin were replaced by Burton and the East Belt Line. Calvin was entering a new era of challenge, crisis, and change. Ironically, as Calvin moved to a campus almost idyllically isolated and apparently sealed from the potentially explosive neighborhood it was leaving, the word most loudly and frequently heard on the new campus was *involvement*. In this new place, the old faith was asked to illuminate and influence a new day, to shed light on the passion-packed issues of the times, to be "relevant" to students who wanted immediate answers largely derived from current thought. The shift of the college was going to involve more than a locality.

The sixties constituted one of the angriest decades in American history. Anger at the war in Vietnam and anger at those angered by the war, rage between the races, wrath at social injustice, none of it contained, seethed across the land. The pictures remain etched in our minds: the blocks of burning cities, three magnetic person-alities assassinated, Alabama sheriffs with their dogs and hoses, the mindless wreckage at Columbia University, the gun-toting students marching out of Cornell, the bloody harvest at Kent State, the police confrontations with the radical left, and the littered agony in Vietnam. The cry "non-negotiable" filled the air as extravagant demands were extravagantly made. The great promises of the Johnson administration had failed to come true, but they had triggered a social concern in many students. Calvin College did not escape these stresses. Violent confrontation was nonexistent, but the anger in the nation hovered over the campus and at times burst into violent expression of conviction and opinion.

It is always difficult to date a new era exactly, but the intellectual shock of the orbiting of "Sputnik" in 1958 affected Calvin as well as other American colleges. Following this event there were many notable changes in attitudes toward education and in the patterns of education. Students gradually grew more critically outspoken, less subservient to authority, and more self-oriented than formerly. By 1962, as Calvin began its shift to the Knollcrest campus, the new temper was apparent; by 1966 it was noisily inescapable; and in 1968-69 it probably reached a climax which relaxed but slightly until 1972. This temper greatly affected the intellectual and spiritual life of the college; it was often effectively and noisily expressed in *Chimes* and *Dialog*, from whence its utterances frequently and abrasively permeated every facet of public relations. The passion for involvement sometimes led to extreme reactions, such as that expressed by the editor of *The Banner*, who complained that "the controlling philosophy of Calvin leads to an accommodating attitude toward unbelievers, in which the Lordship of Christ is ignored." This, to the best of my knowledge, was an erroneous assessment of the administration and faculty, but there were articles in the school papers which could be adduced to prove it true of some of the students. Such statements and those by other individuals and one hostile organization led to suspicion, mistrust, and even attacks. The rhythm of ideas never seems to observe metrical rules and the emotions behind them burst the proper beat.

The signs of the new mood came large and clear in 1962. In the years following, Calvin became ever more involved in the culture and events of the day. Dr. Lewis Smedes in 1962 became president of the Urban League. The *Chimes* insisted that we must be active in the community and concerned with "migrant workers and Negroes." The KIDS Program, to which many Calvin students devoted countless hours, was organized. Mission Emphasis Week focused on "Christ in the City," with the Manhattan missionaries as speakers. Calvin College and Aquinas, a local Catholic college, sought closer contact, especially in the discussion of philosophy and theology. Calvin students and professors appeared on a local television program *Ten O'clock Scholar*. In 1964 some students joined the protest march in Selma, Alabama; in 1967, sixteen students joined protest marches in Washington, D.C. Students and faculty spoke out on the use of the bomb in Vietnam, conscientious objectors, and race relations. The relationship between the antithesis and involvement was hard to define.

The new mood did not leave campus life itself untouched. School rules were attacked as Puritanic. Editor Harold Bontekoe of *Chimes* says:

> The college seems to consider the study and mastery of Emily Post to be equally important as the work of Plato and Aristotle.

This bit of hyperbole underlies the mood. The "anti-liquor laws" of the college came under attack, although student use of liquor was seldom staggering. The Film Council became active and the films often controversial. Rock music, the successor to rock and roll, which a student in 1957 had criticized as music "which is calculated to stir up the wildest, lowest passions," was widely listened to on records and tapes. The Beats came on with a lot of noise and a mouthful of sentimental slush. Even the humor changed. A *Chimes* editor called for a "fierce idea of humor," and the surreptitiously published *Bong* with its plethora of puns and grotesque cartoons responded. *Prism* no longer devoted itself to college life but gave us commanding shots of Ford, Agnew, Julian Bond, Father Groppi, as well as local shots of such gripping subjects as the Pantlind Hotel, Schlitz Beer, telephone wires, traffic lights, and other local wonders. In 1961 the Saturday chapel was dropped; chapel was held three times a week, and faculty members spoke once a week. There was a good deal of provincial and bombastic criticism of our ethnic heritage, and a lot of gaseous piffle about our "Christian Reformedness." This criticism came from the youth of our church trained in our tradition and in our churches and schools. In criticizing the temper of these students, people often forgot that "the buck does not stop" at Calvin College.

This chapter is very difficult to write because of the recency of the events, the plethora of data, the visceral nature of the debates on complex issues, and the fact there are one hundred and fifty faculty observers, who have their own notions about the way it was. It is therefore only an attempt to detect and relate some cardinal patterns on a crowded canvas.

The years 1962-1974 teemed with activity in stone and steel as well as in thought, feeling, and action. The college had first to accommodate itself to a split campus and then to move to a permanent one. The enrollment rose from 2,537 in 1962 to 3,575 in 1968, a high point in enrollment. During these years there was a gruelling search for new faculty members, who often had an imperial array of offers to choose from. One candidate for a position in the English Department had eleven offers. He did not choose ours. The Psychology Department had the hardest task, and Dr. John Daling for years taught immensely large classes. An enormous amount of faculty and administrative time was consumed by response to student agitation. Two major efforts at reorganization took place. The revision of the curriculum is discussed in another chapter. The reorganization of the government of the college is propounded in a document entitled "A Proposal Concerning the Governance of the College." This eighty-two-page document represents hours upon hours of hard work by FOSCO (the Faculty Organization Study Committee), and its discussion, often interminable, is not yet complete. If the faculty adopts it, the college will be organized as never before. Finally, in 1975 a Presidential Search Committee was appointed to present to faculty and Board candidates for the replacement of President Spoelhof, who retires in 1976.

Moving the college, even for only four miles, was a complicated and often uncomfortable process. There were 160,000 books in the library to be transported, in addition to the card files. The latter presented a difficult problem since the cards in the Hekman Memorial Library were combined under subject matter and title, whereas these entries were split in the new library. The price of professional movers was steep; so the college rented a truck and with student help moved all the books and files in a period of three weeks. The books were carefully placed on book carts in the order of the Hekman Library stacks, then loaded onto a truck, and finally arranged in the identical order on the new stacks. The split campus with which Calvin lived for ten years involved students and faculty shuttling from one area to the other. The split campus meant separate chapels and separated administrative offices, and many students had to bustle about on old buses, some of which had had a million miles of service. One was so weary that it occasionally had to be pushed into action. By 1966 one-third of the students were housed and largely taught on the new campus. By the early seventies the old red buildings were hardly known to most students, and when faculty members spoke of them, the students often felt with Carlyle, "What an enormous magnifier is tradition."

The master plan drawn up by Perkins and Will through the unusual gifts of Mr. Fyfe concretely expressed the academic and spiritual ideals outlined by President Spoelhof. New buildings followed the ones already mentioned: the Physical Education Building in 1965, the Fine Arts Center and four residence halls in 1966, a Student Commons in 1967, the Science Building and two residence halls in 1968. The Library was expanded in 1970 and two residence halls were added. The College Center, containing the Gezon Auditorium, a priceless gift, was ready for use in 1973, the Natatorium, a gift of the Bergsma brothers, was dedicated in 1974. The campus is now admirably equipped to serve four thousand students.

Calvin authorities had been trying to sell the old campus for years. Despite various proposals and tentative inquiries, it remained unsold. Its sale was inevitable, and few had any responsible criticism when it finally was sold in 1972. What little real criticism surfaced was centered on three questions: Why so little money? Why had it not been sold before? Why had it not been retained for denominational use? At one time Calvin had hoped to sell it for at least $3,000,000, but despite intensive advertising there were no real bidders. It was finally sold to the Grand Rapids School of Bible and Music in an intricate financial arrangement because there was no alternative and because the prospective buyer would use the property for spiritual purposes as well as to stabilize the neighborhood. The church was not interested in using the buildings, and Calvin could not afford "important and imaginative uses for an idle campus." Anyone who visits the old campus will note the careful grooming it receives, the extensive and expensive rehabilitation it has experienced, and the prepossessing appearance and cordiality of both student body and faculty. Whatever Calvin lost was gained by the community.

This shift to the new campus involved a series of startling contrasts. The Knollcrest campus was fresh, original, organic. Its admirable symmetry was everywhere apparent, the product of a brilliant plan translated into beauty. It provided superbly unified facilities. The old campus with its weathered buildings, its attractive web of traditions, its slow growth characterized by irregularity and inorganic individuality was not easily forgotten by many of the staff. Here for them every room held memories of former teachers and students. Moreover, the mood of the new campus was sharply different. In the last years the old campus had forced the institution into confrontation with deep social problems. One felt them in minor ways as the neighborhood children trampled the green grass on the way to high school in utter disregard of the "Keep Off" signs and roamed through and pilfered in the halls and library. Students themselves faced theft and mugging. Student apartments in the neighborhood were robbed. In the fall of 1970 there were six attacks on students. One was struck on the head; another was slugged on the chin with a hose or pipe. The police dismissed these attacks as caused by a little group of troublemakers. One student who sought to protect himself suggested the use of knives to Dean Lucasse, who replied that "a club or pipe would be more practical." Later on some students were severely beaten. One of the women faculty members who lived a few blocks from the college was robbed three times, once while the thieves tied her to the banister. The Knollcrest campus, in comparison, lay bathed in serenity. Calvin has been criticized for allegedly failing in Christian witness by moving from the area. Though I believe in such witness and though my family and I still live here in this neighborhood, I find it certainly disputable that an educational institution with its highly visible, open, and vulnerable life is under a similar obligation. Protests coming from areas to which the problems are foreign are especially disconcerting.

The fret and ordeal involved in the transitional process affected the administrative staff most severely. The dean of the college had many vexing practical matters to solve. In the initial stages of the process Calvin enjoyed the seasoned service of Dr. Henry J. Ryskamp. However, in 1964, after serving the college twenty-three years as dean and twenty-two years as Professor of Economics, Dr. Ryskamp retired. He had replaced Dean Rooks in 1941; during President Schultze's severe illness he served as acting president, and in 1951 was recommended as one of the candidates for the presidency. As chairman of the Educational Policy Committee, he played an important role in the selection of new faculty members and in the fruitful cooperation with various accrediting agencies. He represented the college at many important academic conferences. His services were manifold and contributed significantly to Calvin's quality.

Dean Ryskamp was a humane and talented scholar, a gracious and poised administrator, modestly but staunchly courageous in presenting his convictions whether at the college or in his writings. In the early thirties his consistent application of Calvinistic principles to social problems drew harsh criticism from some leaders in the church. Though a man of many-sided learning, he had the gift of sympathetic understanding and a generosity in encouragement. One never went to the dean with a thorny problem without receiving a sympathetic hearing and a judicious answer. He had a relaxing sense of humor and the ability to share in that of others. He could unbend without losing dignity. He was the genial sponsor of the short-lived and rather zany Neo-Pickwickian Club, whose members read papers on Tolstoi, Walton, Flaubert, and others in such outlandish places as the attic of the Administration Building, the lobbies of various hotels, and the college basement. He could also preside with manifest effectiveness at august occasions. His sanity, wit, and Christian wisdom enriched the life of the college.

Calvin was also fortunate in the appointment of its new dean, Dr. John Vanden Berg, who succeeded Dr. Ryskamp in 1964. Dean Vanden Berg had served in the Department of Economics with distinction since 1947, and he brought to the office a clear and analytical mind which could identify key problems and suggest workable answers. Before assuming his new office, he had served Grand Rapids as City Commissioner from its Third Ward with marked community approval and appreciation, an office which Dr. Howard Rienstra fills with distinction today. His work in guiding the college through the transition to the 4-1-4 program demonstrated his capacity for arduous effort, balanced insight, skillful planning, and tactful implementation. He attentuated sharp controversy through unruffled continuing friendship. Profoundly interested in the cause of Christian education, he has devoted great efforts to advance it not only at Calvin but in the state and nation through writing and public debate. Ardently committed to Reformed perspectives in education and demonstrating in his personal, ecclesiastical, and academic activities his self-sacrificing devotion to them, he is serving Calvin with dedication and honor.

The president, the new dean, and the faculty soon were challenged and even defied by the new temper of the student body. This temper was not indigenous on the campus and never erupted into the crudity some college campuses encountered because of the Christian spirit and innate decency of the vast majority of the student body and the wise responses on the part of the president, administration, and faculty. The revolt of the young college students in the sixties was unique in the history of American education, and became an immensely discussed social phenomenon. Events outside as well as within the college campuses contributed to its origin and development. The adulatory and permissive attitude of American parents, the bloated means many of them had to indulge their children in unearned luxuries, their own pre-occupation with possessions instead of the spiritual needs of their children contributed to its rise. The promises of the great society, the sharply awakened social conscience, and the unpopular war in Asia accelerated its growth. The students themselves, as Dean Vanden Berg has perceptively said, wanted "immediate answers in immediate contexts," and the schools themselves on all levels often capitulated to the demand for an emphasis on the present. When this generation, hailed as gifted beyond all others, appeared on the college campus, they were inclined to view it as Matthew Arnold viewed Oxford many years before, as a "home of lost causes and forsaken beliefs, and unpopular names, and impossible loyalties." There was often little use in discussing the matter, because everyone's own opinion had become sacred and there was no use at all in echoing Arnold's comment to his niece, "I'm not dogmatic, I'm right." The tremors of adaptation to these new attitudes reverberated over the land.

In 1964 the revolt of the "young intellectual," as it has been called, assumed serious dimensions in the country, and its outermost ripples beat softly on the Calvin campus. The Vietnam war was interwoven through all thought, and the "new maturity" that students sought was heavily prodded by this unpopular war. In the *Prism* of 1966 the process of maturation is still defined in a traditional way. The student, says the *Prism* writer, "attempts this not within the constrictive confines of individualism but always within the criteria of Calvin College and the revealed truth of God." In 1967, however, the new spirit exploded. The criteria of Calvin College were often regarded as restrictive, the revealed truth of God was sometimes boldly and baldly reassessed, and individualism was no longer considered constrictive but intensely liberating. There was a considerable eruption of romantic sentimentalism, of singing and celebrating oneself sometimes reminiscent of Coleridge at his silliest. There was also, however, a sizable group brilliant in thought and expression, spiritually sensitive, and deeply concerned about fundamental social and theological problems. Some of them were, unfortunately, noisy, ill-mannered, and enamored with the tactics of overkill and shock. These students set the tone of student opinion; all had to be taken seriously, especially in the mood of the times. It is from them I quote, and I am trying to quote them fairly and representatively. It should be added that many students were but mildly interested in these matters; some appeared almost uninterested, among them some of the ablest students on campus.

Student opinion was important in four areas: social and moral concerns external to the campus; similar concerns on the campus; academic issues on campus; and reassessment of religious perspectives. The issues cannot be neatly severed, nor do they exhaustively define the tempest, but they do, I think, identify the main blasts.

The concern among students about moral and social issues appeared not only in outspoken outrage against the Vietnam war and racism, but also in invitations to certain speakers to appear on campus. Some of the editorials on these issues were brilliantly written. An editorial on the Vietnam war won statewide recognition, and a documentary on the troubled racial relations at Timothy Christian School by John Ottenhoff was an excellent bit of reporting. The most notorious case of inviting an outside speaker occurred when Mr. Dick Gregory, a comedian and then a crusader for the rights of black minorities, was asked to speak in 1967. Mr. Gregory had been offered a contract to lecture to the college community only. The Board of Trustees cancelled the contract because of "the abrasively vulgar manner of his presentation and style." With heavy sarcasm a student reporter states that "the sanctified stage of the Fine Arts Center is to remain inviolate." The following day there was an anemic demonstration on the steps of the Commons on the old campus with signs such as "Take the Deadwood off the Board of Trustees." *Chimes* publicly offered a list of pen pals among the Board members for letters of protest. One student wrote, "The decision points out who really runs the college"—as if that were or should be a matter of dispute. Later some students attended Gregory's lecture at Hope College and concluded that "his appearance would have benefited the entire Calvin community." This is but a representative incident; the problem in each case was similar.

Many of the moral and social problems hotly discussed by students and, consequently, also by the faculty finally converged on the idea of *in loco parentis*. For decades students had been sent to Calvin as well as other American colleges by parents who felt that the regulations of the college should be designed to create an environment in keeping with parental concern and expectations. This idea assumed that during a student's enrollment the college had a kind of parental authority over him. Some students now became increasingly uncomfortable with this function of the college. Roger Helder in the *Prism* of 1965 says, "The concept of *in loco parentis* is anachronistic, anti-Christian and undemocratic." His is a rather reasonable voice; he does not argue that "students should make policy decisions" but that they should have more participation in the "decision making process," a bulky and very popular phrase. Others became more strident; a student in the halls states, "A growing number of residents insist that they be able to fix their own norms of consideration and concern for others." This author, strangely enough, finds this fault to lie in "Christian administration," an idea of governance he claims incomprehensible. He says:

Somehow Christian administration usually turns into the incul-
cation of a certain culture and a certain life-style in Calvin
College's case, maybe an early 1960's Dutch/God/and country
type of culture . . . . [and] has degenerated into a policy of in
loci uteri, which smacks of self-defense and self-preservation.

The writer resents the fact that the "Residence Hall Staff Manual"
requires counsellors to "build and maintain" an "image of Calvin
College." In the judgment of many students their behavior should
be determined by personal conscience rather than school rules, whether such action involved beer, pot, curfew, church attendance, or other
activities.

The school year 1967-68 was probably the peak of student ac-
tivism, although a real erosion of such action did not begin until
1971. In his report to the Board on February 6, 1968, President
Spoelhof said "everything nailed down seems to come loose." It
was the year of the Dick Gregory episode and other troubles for the
newly formed Lectureship Council. An Ad Hoc Disciplinary Committee was formed to accommodate the growing traffic and student
demands for involvement. Vociferous rumblings about compulsory
chapel filled the air. In this year, for the first time in Calvin's history, an editor of *Chimes* was asked to resign. General Hershey and
his harsh line on the draft agitated the Student Council. Father
Groppi grappled gratingly with grinding social problems. The Honors
Convocation in the spring of 1970, an occasion specifically devoted
to recognizing dispassionate scholarly achievement, was marred by
an intrusive and arrogant student address. However, by the fall of
1970, as the general temper of student revolt waned in the country
and the harsh realities of a less affluent society became apparent, the
unrest began to abate, and on February 1, 1971, President Spoelhof
could report to the Board that "at the present moment it appears
as if we have reached a plateau and the running should by rights
become smoother."

Calvin was spared the violent confrontations on some campuses
because of the wise and conciliatory response of President Spoelhof
and the numerous tactful and balanced actions taken by the administration as a whole as well as by the calming and sane involvement of various faculty members in the problems of the students.
Furthermore, the innate decency and Christian temper of the overwhelming majority of the student body moderated the efforts of the
more raucous elements. It must never be forgotten that a great many
students remained primarily students and sought neither to upset

or politicize the college. In an interview given to the editors of *Chimes,* President Spoelhof said in March 29, 1968, probably the peak year of harsh dissent, that Calvin is interested in "requests upon the administration and the faculty for legitimate change. . . . The faculty would like to look at and assess student questions and suggestions." Sympathetic dialog, acceptable constructive adaptations, the delegation of increased responsibility to students on important committees, particularly those relating to student activities, reduced tensions to manageable proportions. Students were able to participate more fully in the Communications Board and the Discipline Committee. The Student Senate was given increased powers and some of the members were given the floor to express their views on FOSCO, the document dealing with the proposed governance of the college. Many changes in the social and religious life of the college were initiated by students. Not that the most vociferous students were satisfied; they seldom are. In 1969 the effigy of Dean Lucasse was burned to protest an "unclear, undefined, ambiguous disciplinary action." The appearance of FOSCO stimulated further criticism. The school year 1970-71, however, saw a real diminution in tension.

In 1962 a group of younger faculty members who considered the traditional curriculum inadequate for meeting the current challenges or goals of the college began agitation to reconsider and refashion it. Their efforts initiated the consideration and adoption of the 4-1-4 program described in another chapter. Although the process aroused considerable student interest and response, it was essentially a faculty undertaking. The students, however, initiated formal teacher evaluation, convinced that informal assessments were unproductive. The *Chimes* began to insist upon it. Editor Mark Wagenveld says that "the real need of a school is not a large faculty but a good one." Formal evaluation and subsequent publication of the results will "shock teachers out of bad habits." In 1966, Dean Vanden Berg stated that the administration was to prepare evaluation sheets and added that "the primary goal of faculty rating will be improvement of teaching at this college," but that the administration "does not intend to publish its findings." Then followed the massive printing and subsequent distribution of evaluation forms, which, if checked with reasonable care, at least gave an idea as to how students felt about the teaching at Calvin even if many of the weaknesses were irremediable and certain virtues went unnoticed. Faculty compliance was voluntary. Later a good proportion of the faculty consented to publication of the findings. After a few years, interest in the evaluations waned. Faculty evaluation of the evaluations varied from animated approval to unenthusiastic compliance to wan disenchantment with the whole affair. In 1974 they were reintroduced and the computerized results were made available for contemplation, congratulation, or remedial action.

Student opinion, as we have seen, often aroused strong reactions not only in the college but among its supporters. Nowhere was this more evident than in the various student comments on the Reformed faith and the church which professed it. Many examples of such comment can be given, but the essence of the comments and the resulting impact is most strikingly illustrated in a scorching *Chimes* editorial entitled "The Great Gap," April 22, 1966. This article asserted the presence of an immense chasm between intellectually virile students and their traditions. Systematic theology, once useful, is now "sterile, strait-jacketed by remote abstractions." The answer is to "chuck every theological abstraction" and to "start theologizing all over again," "to learn to read Scripture like any other book," even though it is inspired, "to treat it with the best historical and literary tools available." The community should stop heresy-hunting. "There is no such thing as heresy," announces the author. "There are only Christians and non-Christians." We must tie "legalism to the hanging tree." Since the entire piece was written with a good deal of literary skill, its impact was immense. These highly inflammable sentiments, in no way endorsed by the faculty or the majority of the student body, were immediately pounced upon by critics of the college, who, often for their own purposes, tend to treat such atypical utterances as representative. The Publication Committee acted promptly and published a statement of its own position in the *Chimes,* reasserting Calvin's traditional insistence that all writing in the school publications "must reflect a living and thoughtful Reformed Christian perspective on life," and that "all student writing shall be consistent with a loyalty to the Scripture, particularly, as interpreted in the Reformed confessions." It demanded an apology from the editor of *Chimes* and a public reaffirmation of his agreement with these principles.

Some of the reaction to student challenges, or presumed challenges, to traditional religious beliefs appeared frankly and openly in *The Banner* and in other periodicals; some of it was conducted in semi-clandestine fashion through privately circulated bills of complaint and speeches before selected audiences. Particularly active in

this guerrilla warfare was the Association of Christian Reformed
Laymen, a self-appointed C.I.A. of the church militant, dedicated to
the detection and eradication of whatever they have thought erroneous. The attacks were damaging to both the image and the budget of
the college. Some of the reactions of the general public were under-
standable. When a loyal supporter of the college reads in *Chimes* that
"the Christian life at Calvin is a cliche itself . . . . a dull, apathetic,
half-dead affair," or in even stronger language, "Talk about 'Reformed Principle' now seems irrelevant or at best forced. The ideas
which were once identified as the product of Reformed principles
have lost currency in our college," one can understand the bewilderment and even anger, particularly when such sentiments recur and
the reader thinks he sees a figure in the carpet. Furthermore, the
nature and currency of these ideas were magnified by rumor, and
the attempts by the college to contain, modify, and correct them
were consistently ignored or minimized by hostile critics of the college.

Nowhere is the change in student attitude and temper from
the fifties to the sixties better illustrated than in student publications,
even though they are not wholly representative. The writers of the
fifties had a genuine interest in propositional theology, an awareness
of and regard for Reformed tradition, a pervasive politeness, and a
critical approach constructively loyal to the ideals of the college. The
writers of the late sixties reacted against propositional theology,
showed little knowledge of tradition, and seemed disenchanted with
what they did know. Coming out of Christian homes and Christian
schools, they seemed to me surprisingly patterned by naturalistic and
pragmatic perspectives. I remember a class discussion in which a
bright student argued boldly for reforming society through "human
engineering," a concept, as he argued it, based wholly on naturalistic
psychology. It was indeed an opportunity to put the college catalog
into action, "to cultivate in the student value-judgments related to
a thorough knowledge of facts about man's relation to God . . . .
and to his fellowman" in the light of the "creedal position of the
denomination," but it was done in a rather chilly atmosphere. The
mood of the day was dissent and innovation, and the lack of interest in "creedal positions" was obvious even in many Christian students who found emotion more appealing than doctrinal precision.

All these contentious activities deeply affected the life of the
college. Students not only expressed themselves on the war, drugs,
rock, and chapel, but also emphasized their right to help decide the
nature of their education and the methods by which it should be

accomplished. They inveighed against the idea of a "spoon-fed infant in college," preferring at times to take over the feeding themselves. The mood was analytical and critical, not synthetic; there was little disinterestedness in the approach. I am fully aware that many of the students saw these days as bursting with excitement and challenging reexamination, the air filled with the pleasant burning of old wood. Doctrine can become ornament instead of architecture, merely external instead of part of the life of the structure. Yet in a deeper sense most of the writing and action will be a "moment's monument," as old truths come back into fashion. By 1971 much of the sound and fury was subsiding. Throughout these years many of the younger members of the faculty were particularly helpful in restraining and revising student thinking and action. President Spoelhof also deserves high praise for dealing courageously and successfully with many very difficult situations. Neither was the student movement without idealism and insight, which when winnowed from the chaff contributed to the development of the college.

One old problem, however, resurfaced in a new form. In the twenties and the thirties the church and consequently the college were insolubly vexed by the question of movie attendance. In 1961, Synod decided that movies are not always sinful in themselves and that they may therefore be discriminately attended. When Synod reached that decision, they sang the doxology. Warnings about attending improper movies were solemnly uttered; but discrimination is a large word, and it allowed enough stretching so that the problem evaporated at the college in the sixties, although faculty members who went discriminately to the movies still wondered who might see them go. In 1966, Synod forged ahead and adopted a report "The Church and the Film Arts," in which it stated that the film is "a legitimate cultural medium to be used by the Christian in the fulfillment of the cultural mandate." It stated, furthermore, that mature Christians are "to exercise a responsible personal freedom in the use of the film arts." Somehow "film arts" acts like an antiseptic. Furthermore, Synod said that there should be a "constructive critique of the film arts" through which "specialists in art and Christian ethics" give leadership to the church and society. President Spoelhof on September 28, 1966, called a meeting of approximately twenty-five faculty members to discuss this decision and then appointed an eight-member Focus Committee to determine policy and action. The committee proposed that all the faculty make themselves critically aware of films, especially those shown in the course Christian Perspectives on Learning. The committee also recommended the formation of a Calvin Film Council, which included among its duties the formation of a procedure by which films would be critically discussed as well as shown on campus.

Since 1967 the Calvin Film Council has attempted to rent reputable films for campus viewing. The chosen films were generally previewed by a committee drawn from the faculty and student body, a costly and time-consuming experience. Many excellent films have been shown; some, however, legitimately considered to be examples of film art, embodied a moral dimension not immediately perceptible or otherwise easily susceptible of misinterpretation. Such films included "Bonnie and Clyde," "La Dolce Vita," and most recently "Caberet." In each case there was vocal criticism. Unfortunately, not all questionable films were viewed in the framework of Christian contextual criticism and not all viewers remained to be enlightened. Doubtless, as Professor Slenk says, it is an unfair responsibility for "a student-led committee to shoulder this academic burden," and it sometimes made mistakes; but if one considers the many films chosen, the entire program has been a tribute to the intelligence and moral sense of the successive committees. The work of the Film Council, like the editing of *Chimes* or *Dialog,* is difficult, and a fair judge realizes that in each case there is the calculated risk inevitable in an educational institution.

The fevered pace of these crowded years was sharply broken seven times by death in the college community, and each case was marked by singular poignancy in loss and sorrow. On the evening news of a sunny May day, I heard that a boy in my afternoon class but a few hours before had drowned in a little lake outside the city. Later in the week I came upon his term paper, a desolating experience. A few years later a student was drowned in Lake Michigan. One thinks not only of the young lives suddenly obliterated, but of the immeasurable shock to parents hundreds of miles distant, and no way to blunt the piercing of the sword. The sorrow and pain of the parents was shared by the college.

Dr. Lambert Flokstra, Professor of Education at Calvin for more than thirty years, died in the spring of 1965 after serving Christian education in various capacities for almost fifty years. He was just four weeks from a retirement anticipated with many plans. He had served Calvin College as an excellent scholar and meticulous teacher. He was an unusually perceptive thinker. Somewhat distant and formal in the classroom, he could unbend among his friends, where his sense of humor, engaging friendliness, and incisive remarks revealed a dimension not well known to his students. He spent a lifetime in self-sacrificing loyalty to the Kingdom of Christ and its causes.

Dr. John De Vries, an uncommonly gifted and popular teacher, died in the fall of 1967. A teacher who could have taught in many colleges, he chose to spend his talents at Calvin. Shortly after being appointed as Professor of Chemistry, he said in an interview in *Chimes,* in June 1940:

> During my seven years as instructor in two public colleges of this country, I was impressed by the lack of a guiding principle, a moral-religious force in the lives of young people who studied with me.

To furnish his students with such guiding principles became his goal at Calvin, a goal which he pursued with zeal and outspoken convictions. He had the gift of popularizing learning and did so most significantly in his book *Beyond the Atom.* Casual, informal, and hearty in manner, frank and winning in company, completely indifferent to facades and roles, given to banter as well as profoundly religious comment, he was a man of stature and pervasive spiritual influence.

Four years later, in the fall of 1971, Dr. Tony Brouwer, Professor of Economics, died after a long illness from which there was never a point of return. In this illness he strikingly revealed the "Christian faith effective in his life-style," as one of his close friends put it. He lived affirmatively even in the shadow of death, and in his weakness through grace gave strength to those to whom he was dear. His deep faith in the long days of his dying has been made into a moving film. He was not only an able and influential teacher, but an active worker in the cause of the deprived and oppressed, spending himself compassionately in the interests of the common man, whose cause he uncompromisingly championed.

Mr. Leonard Vander Lugt, who taught at Calvin for a relatively short time, also died in the fall of 1971, still a young man. He had proved himself to be an able teacher of chemistry and endeared himself to his students by a marked concern with their intellectual and spiritual progress. A gifted athlete in his younger years, he maintained a strong interest in sports at Calvin. He spent many hours serving the church as well as the school. Genial and winning in personality, deeply concerned with the relations between faith and learning, he sought at all times to strengthen the faith of his students.

Dr. Harmon Hook, Assistant Professor of English, died in the spring of 1974. Having undergone a desperately serious operation a year before, he struggled heroically to overcome its unshakeable consequences. His unswervingly brave struggle to regain health, his good cheer in the face of desperate odds, his utter commitment to God's love and care even in discomfort and pain, made us all aware of the greatness of his spirit and the grace of his Lord. Young, brilliant, admirable in character, he impressed us deeply, and his long illness and death grieved us all. An unusually gifted and articulate scholar, an excellent teacher, and a very productive committee member, he appeared ready for a life of rich service. In the short time the Lord gave him in a providence he gladly surrendered to, he enriched the college community through his faith as well as his learning.

I have interrupted the narrative with these sombre yet hopeful details not only because the services of these men were worth noting, but because each made a memorable impression upon the college community because of the vibrancy of his faith. Their lives, their learning, and their faith moved the faculty to prayer, deep sympathy, and many acts of kindness. The Fine Arts Chapel was crowded for a moving service of prayer for Dr. Hook in his acute illness. These men died in the faith, and the friends who stood beside the grave when they were buried looked far beyond it to a city where such loss and sorrow are unknown. We knew and believed at that sad moment what the ever present Lord had said, "I am the resurrection and the life: he that believeth in me, though he were dead, yet shall he live."

By the early seventies what could be considered as normalcy in the light of the preceding years returned. The 4-1-4 was being adjusted to fit some tight programs. The prolonged analysis and discussion of the document on the governance of the college was inching along. The interim courses because of their variety or intensity of study met with wide approval. Athletic programs achieved notable success. In 1969, Calvin, despite the absence of football, won the All Sports Award in the Michigan Intercollegiate Athletic Association. Calvin won its first M.I.A.A. baseball championship in 1970 under Coach Marv Zuidema, whose soccer teams won championships in four out of the five years from 1970 to 1974. Women's sports soared in popularity and achievement; the women's basketball team coached by Doris Zuidema (neither Marv Zuidema's wife nor sister) won state championships in 1972-1974; her volley-ball teams were similarly successful. The physical education program was greatly strengthened, especially through the addition of the Bergsma Natatorium. Calvin's basketball teams continued their stellar success, and at this writing have won twenty-five consecutive games in the M.I.A.A. under Coach Ralph Honderd. The faculty was strengthened by twenty-one new appointees in 1969, the greatest acquisition of personnel in one year in the history of the college. Extracurricular activities in the arts and the press flourished. There were no major pranks, but there were a few streakers, who could find no better ways of self-expression. Yet the new normalcy was troubled with omens that cast worrisome shadows over the future of Calvin and other private colleges.

The omens of that future were ironically surfacing in the school year 1969-1970, when Calvin had just appointed a record number to the staff. In 1970 the enrollment dipped slightly further from the 1968 peak of 3,575 to 3,437. In 1972 it dropped to 3,185. Intimations of the coming recession were appearing. Teaching positions at all levels and over the entire country were becoming difficult to obtain. For many superbly trained Ph.D.'s there was a depression. Sensing the altering needs of society, students frequently altered their course pro-grams, and entering students majored in fields where positions were available. Some departments, therefore, moved from abundance to scarcity, whereas others became unusually crowded. The mood in the fall of 1971 was tinged with apprehension as a meticulously assembled faculty with high credentials faced the possibility of oversupply. For a time staff vacancies were not continued and replacements were halted. However, through vigorous recruiting in the field and by tele-phone on campus, the decline was arrested and the enrollment slowly rose to 3,414 in the fall of 1974. Maintaining this enrollment in the years ahead will be difficult as the cost of college education inexorably rises year after year and as a disappointing eighteen percent of Chris-tian Reformed young people of college age choose to attend our col-leges. More consumer-oriented courses may have to be introduced and a larger proportion of non-Christian Reformed students will have to be attracted to Calvin. These now number a highly desirable fif-teen percent of the student body.

Calvin College in 1975 is a strong institution. The physical plant is esthetically appealing, commodious, and functional. It draws extra-ordinary support from a loyal constituency, which in addition to per-sonal gifts contributed $1,778,000 in 1974 to the college through the quota system. In addition Calvin enjoys the magnificent support of the State of Michigan through its tuition grants to students who attend private colleges. Many other gifts and grants combined with skillful management have kept the college fiscally sound. Its student body, which compares very favorably with that of other American colleges, is served by a staff of one hundred and fifty-nine full-time teachers and many part-time teachers who together total a staff of twelve more.

The college received praise from a reviewing team of the North Central Association in the spring of 1971 for exhibiting "strong leadership, continued financial stability, and a very able faculty." It is a fine school to serve, as Dr. Edwin Van Kley stated in an article in *The Banner:*

> Academic excellence, respect for scholarship, close personal contact with challenging colleagues, all permeated by a vital Christian faith: these are more successfully achieved at Calvin than at any other place I know. I am grateful to be part of this exciting community.

I think these good words of our colleague speak for us all.

Since the fall of 1951 the college has been led in a remarkable way by President William Spoelhof. His accomplishments, as these pages have shown, have been many, and they have had unusual public appreciation by the faculty, board, and student body. He has insisted upon searching out, appointing, and maintaining the best staff available; he has shown singular devotion to and aptitude for architectural excellence on the campus; he has enthusiastically supported innovative curricular changes; he has defended the college in courageous and diplomatic ways against numerous, and often unfounded and intemperate attacks. Through openness in attitude and persuasive involvement in their ideas and problems, he has won the confidence of the student body. He was always happy to assist faculty members in obtaining grants and fellowships and took great pleasure in their success. Magnanimity and graciousness marked his comments to retiring faculty members. Despite his multifarious duties he consistently involved himself compassionately in the sorrows, illnesses, and bereavements in the faculty family. His convocation addresses set a noble spiritual tone for the new school year. His selfless devotion to the goals of the college increased its prestige and placed an ineffaceable stamp on its character. He has been an uncommonly gifted president during uncommonly difficult years.

Since President Spoelhof is to retire in January of 1976, the Synod of 1974 approved a procedure for the appointment of the president of Calvin College, which required the formation of a Presidential Search Committee, consisting of five members of the Board of Trustees, four members of the college faculty, and two alumni to serve as representatives of the constituency. This committee solicited suggestions for the presidency from all segments of the Calvin constituency. It received one-hundred and fifty names, sixty-two of which were different from any others. From this gross list, thirteen were asked for interviews and ten accepted. After the interviews were conducted and supporting recommendations were received, the committee recommended to the faculty the names of Dr. Anthony J. Diekema, Associate Chancellor and Associate Professor at the University of Illinois Medical School in Chicago, and Dr. Nicholas P. Wolterstorff, Professor of Philosophy at Calvin College. The committee considered both candidates eminently qualified in "Reformed convictions," "admirable character," educational achievement, cultural awareness, and the capacity of communicating the ideals of the college. The faculty endorsed these sentiments and the Board of Trustees recommended both candidates to Synod, which on June 18, by a vote of 82-64, chose Dr. Anthony J. Diekema as the new president of Calvin College.

In the fall of 1906 the catalog of John Calvin Junior College asserted the goal of the college to consist in giving all instruction

> in harmony with Reformed Principles. The various branches of study, therefore, are considered from the standpoint of faith and in the light of Calvinism as a life-and-world view. Herein lies the distinctive character of our College.

This perennially avowed and monumentally complex educational ideal, together with the staff and student body who have sought and seek to realize it, constitutes the uniqueness of Calvin College. To maintain this uniqueness in a Reformed community fragmented by various voices, and in a culture radically hostile to and even contemptuous of it, to continue to acquire a staff both keenly aware of its Reformed heritage and highly competent in scholarship, and to attract students sensitive and loyal to this ideal will be an heroic undertaking ever in need of an abundant presence of God's grace.

CHAPTER NINE

MASTERPIECE OR MENACE? THE 4-1-4

These three numbers mean nothing to most people, but to the administration and faculty of Calvin College, they embody an enormous denotative and connotative resonance. The Curriculum Study Committee, appointed in the spring of 1963, met over one hundred times before the report "Christian Liberal Arts Education," written by Nicholas Wolterstorff, appeared in October 1965. The faculty had extensive and frequent open hearings on the report before it was adopted. Departments spent many hours, not always relaxed, in fashioning new programs to meet its new patterns, and the Educational Policy Committee met sixty-six times before these new programs were approved. Here I am reminded of a seminary professor who joined in haying in Iowa during the summer. His host remarked, "I see you can work too." All this strenuous activity was carried on by a faculty still teaching twelve to fifteen hours, often with bulging classes. When Professor Boer made his inaugural speech, his motto was *Per ardua ad astra*. There was here absolutely no doubt about the *ardua;* it is the *astra* that raises the $64,000 question.

These laborious discussions and studies were not forced upon the faculty by an accrediting agency. In fact, as we have seen, the North Central Review Team had said on November 17, 1961:

> Calvin College has developed an enviable reputation as a first-class liberal arts college where students, faculty and administration together reach a high level of academic achievement. The review team believes the record is deserved.

The studies arose not out of dissatisfaction with academic performance, but out of doubt as to whether the current curriculum constituted the best possible mode of achieving the educational goals of the college. Was the current curriculum the best academic means to stimulate the student "to offer his whole creative, imaginative, intellectual and social enterprise eagerly and earnestly in the services of God and his fellowman, thereby acknowledging the lordship of Christ over all things?" Did it most adequately provide an education "governed by the Christian faith as reflected in the Reformed standards?" Such were the questions a number of the younger faculty members asked. They found the curriculum wanting. After a number of informal discussions, they brought their concern to the faculty and convinced them of the validity of their discontent. A Curriculum Committee was appointed in 1963, and in 1965 it submitted its report to the faculty.

President Spoelhof in his "Preface" to *Christian Liberal Arts Education* calls the faculty meetings exclusively devoted to analyzing and debating this report in 1965-66 "the most exciting, dramatic and proudest moments we ever experienced as a faculty." I suppose most of the supporters of the new curriculum would agree. Furthermore, if the meetings deserved these superlatives, it is partly true because President Spoelhof encouraged frank and open discussion and Dr. Wolterstorff fielded all questions with courtesy and understanding. Agreement with the committee's report whether in the theoretical section or in the practical applications was neither instantaneous nor unanimous. One faculty member, impatient with the discussion, said, "It is harder to move a college than a cemetery." Every faculty member could voice his convictions, whether he regarded the new program as a masterpiece or a menace. Furthermore, all major changes had to receive a two-thirds vote. Consequently, there was little debris in the way of rancor and a great deal of sincere cooperation by the loyal opposition in implementing the new program.

The liberal arts curriculum at Calvin had often been altered and augmented, but its adequacy for the peculiar needs of a Calvinistic institution had never received profound or prolonged discussion until 1965. Calvin had tried over the years to give a liberal arts education at once nonutilitarian yet very useful, an education achieving its Calvinistic character not through a unique pattern of courses but by applying in them a unique perspective. The faculty had from the beginning a distaste for professional or specialized training; its heart lay in the liberal arts program. Former President Broene stated in his inaugural address in 1926:

> College is a place for instruction in the liberal arts not in the professions. . . . Surely, we want to give mathematics a place of honor but not engineering.

Furthermore, he deprecates giving college credit for courses in teacher training, even though Calvin had a sizable portion of its student body enrolled in such studies. He says in the same address:

> Doubtless, circumstances will force us to give in, but if so, then
> we must endeavor to keep all professional training to an irre-
> ducible minimum.

His statements dramatize Calvin's early insistence on the importance
of the liberal arts in the college and help explain the priority of the
reexamination of the liberal arts curriculum in 1962. Today, however, even though Calvin insists upon remaining a first-class liberal
arts college, the greatly increased number of preprofessional and professional students and the pressure to accelerate the introduction of
other professional programs pose difficult problems in relating the
various professional courses of study effectively and harmoniously to
a liberal arts emphasis. Calvin must continue to insist, I should
think, that the college stimulate and nurture what is universal in
man as man whatever specialized studies will be offered. This will
be hard to insist upon in a pragmatic society in which specific adaptation is considered highly important, and in a democratic society
in which one subject is assumed to be as important as any other.

The liberal arts curriculum which Calvin offered in 1921 was
intended to be an important means by which the institution hoped
to achieve its ideal as stated in the catalog in 1921 and found in
successive catalogs until very recently:

> The aim of the college is to give young people an education
> that is Christian, in the larger and deeper sense that all class
> work, all the student's intellectual, emotional, and imaginative
> activities shall be permeated with the spirit and teaching of
> Christianity.

Calvin's curriculum was, however, borrowed, not specifically designed
by the faculty to fit the unique goals of the institution. With the
exception of eight hours of Bible, which had to be ingeniously renamed to be acceptable for admission to the graduate school, the
faculty simply borrowed the curriculum of the University of Michigan, doubtless, in all fairness, in order to secure accreditation. Furthermore, in addition to Bible, all candidates for the A.B. had to
take six hours of rhetoric, six of history, six of psychology and logic,
six of philosophy, twelve of French or German, and ten of science.
The remaining hours fulfilled majors, minors, and electives. The
program allowed a very sizable variety of courses, particularly if the
student took a few extra hours each semester.

This curriculum was in force at Calvin for liberal arts students

until 1967, and students in the increasingly numerous pre-professional programs had to meet its requirements if they wished to receive an A.B. Although there was a great deal of animated and sometimes acrimonious discussion about the adoption of new courses, there was next to no discussion about the validity of the entire liberal arts curriculum until the middle fifties. There was, indeed, prolonged discussion of the pre-seminary requirements, but these discussions arose out of linguistic fatigue by students who had long muttered about the heavy requirements in Greek and Dutch, the extreme tightness of the program, and the difficulty in being admitted to the graduate school on its basis. After several full days of meetings at the Knollcrest Manor House in 1957, the language requirements were modified and the courses so arranged that a pre-seminary student could receive a regular A.B. degree. Serious assessment of the adequacy of the curriculum was initiated by Dr. Jellema after his return from the University of Indiana. In 1958 he published the monograph "The Curriculum in a Liberal Arts College." This little book provided an incisive analysis of the whole problem, and its insights and concrete suggestions, though not adopted by the committee, remain relevant and thought-provoking.

In this monograph Dr. Jellema contends that if "education is for wisdom" in the deepest Calvinistic sense, Calvin's curriculum fails because it does "not curricularly insure liberal education." The intrinsic idea of its curriculum is that "wisdom consists very simply in the ability so to use nature as to achieve position in a society devoted to mastery over nature." The wisdom that Calvin's traditional curriculum yields is naturalistic. In the first two years only Bible and history acquaint the student curricularly with a different mind, and then only if the right history course is chosen; in the latter years the only required subjects that insure the same end are philosophy and more Bible. Obviously, this implies that a teacher will have an arduous task in utilizing such intractable material to further the Calvinistic ideals of the college. The subject matter does not inherently advance the educational goals of the college.

Dr. Jellema insists that a curriculum which aims at "the man of God completely furnished" have an intrinsic design that would insure such a goal. Such a curriculum would acquaint the student with the mind a Christian man ought to think with, the fundamental perspectives that should determine his entire way of looking at life. It also makes the student aware of the minds in opposition to such thinking. Consequently, Dr. Jellema says flatly:

No student is liberally educated who is not familiar from the inside with the Pagan Mind, both on its idealistic and materialistic side, the Christian Mind (Middle Ages and the Reformation), and the Renaissance-Contemporary Mind.

A curriculum which insures this will "make the antithesis articulate" because it will not only acquaint the student with the Christian Mind in its deepest dimensions but force him to judge other minds in its terms. Whether the student confronts the modern mind webbed in the system of nature or the classical mind limited to the rational or humanistic dimensions, he will meet them with the basic commitments of the Christian mind.

Dr. Jellema then presents a concrete pattern of courses designed to fill the needs of a Christian liberal education. The proposed curriculum would assure the student's acquaintance with the major minds through courses specifically focused upon them. It would also insist that six of the fourteen hours in *Minds* use primary classics as texts. Such study would be prerequisite to admission to the Senior College in which the student would develop his major, minor and electives. Finally, no senior should graduate without demonstrable efficiency in using a foreign language in his course work.

These proposals were radical and also persuasively cogent, but the pamphlet never received serious faculty discussion. The Curriculum Study Committee states that:

Though his [Jellema's] report did not at the time receive its just consideration, the present report must count his among its significant and stimulating antecedents.

In addition to this laconic reference, the committee acknowledges indebtedness to an essay by Dr. Jellema on "Calvinism and Higher Education" and to an essay by Dr. Henry Zylstra on "Christian Education," both of which insist upon the necessity of Christian perspectives in fashioning a student so that he can live and work "in the Kingdom of God as this is manifest in contemporary society."

The book *Christian Liberal Arts Education* embodies lucidly and succinctly the work of the committee. It was written by Dr. Wolterstorff, whom President Spoelhof calls "the chief architect of our effort," and also owes much to Dr. Charles Miller, whom President Spoelhof calls "the chief engineer of our study." It is a highly stimulating and sizable study serving both the needs of the faculty and those who look to Calvin for a philosophy of education. Obviously, I cannot do justice to it in this account, and I am limiting myself to

its major thrust in theory and suggested implementation.

After an incisive account of the historical background of liberal arts education, the book deals briefly with the American college including Calvin. Christian education, it avers, does not consist in preparation for a flight from life, nor a genteel contemplation of it, nor a successsful adaptation to it. Christian education proceeds from faith, instructs according to its imperatives and helps in maturing a student to live the Christian life in the world. The study rejects a pragmatic curriculum because it is wrongly based, excessively practical, and lacking in historical context. It rejects the classical view, "enormously attractive" though it is, "because it implies passivity on the part of the student and overemphasis on intellectual and cultural history."

The book then develops and recommends a view which it calls, "though not very felicitously," the "disciplinary view." In the disciplinary view of education,

> The primary focus of a Christian liberal arts education . . . [is] on teachers and students together engaging in various scholarly disciplines, directed and enlightened in their inquiries by the Word of God.

This, incidentally, has been the focus of education at Calvin College from the beginning. Whatever the actual or proposed curriculum, Calvin teachers have always tried to share their scholarship with students willing and able to do so. The superiority of the proposed curriculum would have to consist in its ability to make this goal intrinsic to the curriculum, something which the old curriculum did not do. The real contention of the committee was that its distribution of required or *core* courses, the departmental pattern of courses, and "most importantly," in its own words, the course "Christian Perspectives on Learning" would provide a better vehicle for a Christian liberal arts education than the old curriculum did.

Since the book has a good deal to say about "disciplines," one should note what it means by a discipline. It is defined as "the scientific (theoretical) study of some aspect or segment of reality." The book has many worthwhile and subtle things to say about the proper discrimination of disciplines and their interrelation. A discipline, furthermore, is a disinterested, theoretical study of this segment of reality; it may have important practical results but the justification of its study does not lie in "restrictive practical aims." All the disciplines, whether mathematics, history, music, or some other study, are to be pursued "under the guidance of Biblical revelation." A proper pattern of disciplines in conjunction with the *competences*—Speech, Freshman English, elementary foreign languages, the course "Christian Perspectives on Learning," and one unit of physical education—will, it was hoped, provide a curriculum which insures a Christian Liberal Arts Education.

The new curriculum requires the student to take 36 courses or units plus three Interims in four years, instead of the 125 hours traditionally required, on the assumption that four courses a semester instead of five or six will insure, or at least encourage, more depth in each course. Since it would simultaneously reduce the loads of teachers, it would insure, or at least encourage, more preparation, research, and publication. Originally, 19½ courses were contained in the *core,* a pattern of courses required of all candidates for the A.B. This massive course has been adjusted by a consideration of exceptional high school preparation, examinations, and in other ways less easy to comprehend. Now it ranges from 15 to 16½ courses. The remaining courses consist largely of majors, minors, and electives.

The new curriculum also introduced the course "Christian Perspectives on Learning." This course, employing various media and taught interdepartmentally, examines "some contemporary alternatives and challenges to Christianity," and emphasizes Christian perspectives in meeting them. It attempts to lay the ground for "a critical examination of one's academic experience at Calvin College." The committee preferred introducing the course in the senior year despite considerable dissent.

The academic year is now divided into two semesters with an Interim Course between them. The Interim is a seventeen-day period of intensive study of subject matter not normally taught. Innovative and interdisciplinary teaching is encouraged. In the 1973-74 Interim, courses were offered in "The Anatomy of Despair," "The Bones and Stones of the Middle East," "Enameling," "Getting to Know the Birds" and in one hundred and one other subjects. Each student must take three Interims for graduation, one of which must be in his major field.

Calvin College spent Wednesday, May 11, 1967, in acquainting the students with the new curriculum, and it went into operation in the fall of 1967. The transition was smoothly accomplished through the full cooperation of faculty and students and the superb planning of Dean Vanden Berg and Registrar Peter Vande Guchte. During the years 1968 to the present, various changes were introduced, notably in softening the stringency of the *core* requirements. Despite noble resolutions to introduce new courses sparingly, the sharp needs of various areas and new programs have prevented their fulfillment.

Immediate reaction to the introduction of the 4-1-4 was extremely varied both among the faculty and the students. Representative opinions were quoted in two issues of *Chimes* in 1968. These ranged from the assertion that the content of the courses was virtually unchanged and of no greater depth than before to the assertion that some courses, at least, were "completely revised and restructured" and of patently greater depth; from the view that demands upon students were actually lessened to the judgment that they were much harder. I suppose one judges the fair by his own booth. Reactions to the Interim were similarly varied: from "It's easy, it's a good rest" to genuine appreciation of a novel and worthwhile educational experience, whether the students fully exploited their opportunities or loafed through on an *S* (satisfactory). The subterranean, satirical appendix to *Chimes, Bong,* reflecting on the esoteric nature of some of the Interim courses, suggested studies in "The Glory that was Israel" featuring such visual and auditory aids as reenactment of pivotal battles. Another suggestion was "The Semicolon as an Archetypal Motif in the Works of Ogden Nash."

Commenting on "Christian Perspectives on Learning," *Chimes* says the course "received a great deal of praise from both faculty participants and the students who enrolled, who appreciated an opportunity for discussion." One student phrased the idea thus: "We didn't hold anything back—we just said what we believed." The nadir of all comments was, "CPOL is really dumb: all they do is get up there and talk and there's no sense to it." A much more general sentiment was the following: "I've never been brought face to face with why I am going to Calvin College. This was brought out very well in the course."

. Though the majority of the faculty and student body solidly, and in many instances enthusiastically, approved the new curriculum, Professor Gordon Van Harn, a member of the curriculum committee, stated that there were "problem areas that caused some unhappiness." Dean Vanden Berg acknowledged some problems in adjustment but added, "There is more pressure in the new system, frankly that is good." The difficulties or problem areas included the rigidity and size of the *core* and the proper meshing of the new curriculum and the professional and preprofessional programs. Some students were concerned with the presence of too many introductory courses which, probably unfairly, they considered unappetizing repetitions of high school courses. Others felt that the massive *core* jeopardized a solid major. Some teachers felt that the Freshman English and Introductory History courses had been weakened if not wrecked. Finally, there remained the basic question of whether the 4-1-4 curricularly insured a Christian liberal arts education, whether the new pattern of courses noticeably improved the vehicle of instruction in preparing a student to live the Christian life in the world.

In 1972 interested faculty members responded to a lengthy, and in places searching, questionnaire on the validity of the new program. Those who responded solidly approved the "disciplinary view" of liberal arts education; they overwhelmingly agreed that the Interim had genuine values in improving both the content of the curriculum and pedagogical techniques. On a very crucial matter, phrased as follows:

> . . . by reducing the total number of courses . . . . we are reducing the diversity and richness of academic experience.

there was an almost unanimous conviction that it did. The only difference lay in the extent to which faculty members thought it did so; forty-two replied "some" and forty-three, "much." This seems to point up the divided reaction to a very central issue: the choice between diverse academic exposure and intense exposure to limited subject matter.

The same questionnaire encouraged verbal comment in addition to merely checking reactions. These comments are vigorous and perceptive rather than numerous; some boil with disapproval, few grin with approbation. None of the commentators likes the word "disinterested" to describe Christian education. Says one: "I see little justification for undergraduate Christian higher education to be disinterested." Another states that he thinks the faculty adopted the 4-1-4 because of its "catchy arithmetical formula," which "has no meaningful connection with our statement of philosophy." Another feels, echoing the sentiments of some students, that the introductory courses "are watered, are artificial creations." One comments that "a collection of introductions to a discipline, no matter how they are juggled, do not combine to make a general liberal arts education." There are emphatic demands for interdisciplinary courses. All who speak on the matter agree on the importance of a Biblically based religious perspective, although one feels we "ought also to speak of creational revelation." There was a considerable divergence of opinion on the nature, extent, and even value of the core.

These comments cannot be formalized into a systematic critique of the 4-1-4, but they do indicate what I take on the basis of the scarcity of comment from a faculty of one hundred and sixty to be a minority report. If one has no rage to comment, one either affirms the program or is torpid about the whole matter.

It is time to consider the $64,000 question raised at the beginning of the chapter. Was the whole odyssey worthwhile? Is the 4-1-4 really better than the old curriculum? The questions, I believe, are distinct and so are the answers. I think I am stating a fact when I assert that the odyssey was worthwhile. The hard thinking and animated, often profound, discussions, the well-written and stimulating book, the lively experiment—these were all highly profitable. No member of the faculty could fail to come to grips with basic educational problems and fundamental alternatives in meeting them. The second question is much more complex and I should consider myself hopelessly imprudent in attempting to make a judgment. I should only like to make a few observations and point out some fundamental issues that need resolution, always aware that it is difficult to reverse the rotation of a rolling wheel.

The truly rugged questions surface when one evaluates the curricular pattern of the 4-1-4. Do the *core* and other required courses in the program actually provide the best vehicle for a Christian liberal arts education? Does the recommended pattern of courses necessarily result upon adoption of the disciplinary view of education? Does the limitation of courses to four a semester, except in decidedly rare instances, provide an education in depth which compensates for the restricted educational exposure it entails? Should the college permit the average student to take five courses a semester instead of four? Is it sound pedagogical economy to limit the classroom exposure to those who are primarily gifted teachers as the 4-1-4 does? Will the college be able to afford the highly desirable and enjoyable three-course teaching load per faculty member as the economic indicators wobble around at depressing levels and students become harder to attract or recruit? Will it lower literacy standards for admission, soften course requirements for retention, and imperil the heart of the liberal arts program by accommodating it to consumer-oriented offerings in Business English, Wildlife Management, and an infinite variety of courses whirling frothily about the magic word "media"? Whatever choice the faculty makes will I trust be based on rigorous intellectual and spiritual self-study, the discriminative weighing of alternatives, and a profound desire to provide a liberal arts education which will equip students to serve Christ and His Kingdom as well as they can in the culture which they providentially inherit and share.

CHAPTER TEN

LITTLE FOXES IN THE VINEYARD

The leading editorial in the Calvin College *Chimes* of February 1918 is titled "Alarm." Since then, and even before, it has been sounded, and sounded, and sounded. From that year to this, Calvin has rarely been free from suspicion, mistrust, and attack. Few colleges have been more sedulously observed; whenever the torch flickered or somebody thought it did, the trumpet was sounded. Throughout these many years, in mild or vehement ways, the college has been criticized for not being sufficiently aggressive in pulverizing apostasy, for failing to be distinctively or creatively Reformed, for keeping a loose rein on worldliness, for advancing radical ideas or for not advancing them. No facet of college life has escaped: neither the first administration nor the last, nor any in between; neither the faculty nor the student body whether in the statement of opinion or action. All have been assailed more often on the basis of rumor than reality. The criticism has originated in concern and love, but also in hot temper and prejudice. The college community, composed of fallible human beings, has made its share of mistakes and its response to criticism has sometimes been ill-advised and waspish. This chapter records a representative "clamor and clangour" of the "loud alarum bells," and, in so doing, the extreme difficulties in integrating piety and learning.

The amazing feature of the criticism here recorded, which could easily be expanded into a book, is that it is wholly a family affair in which members of the Christian Reformed Church attack fellow members in their employ. This very fact, I suspect, breeds in the critics a sense of sovereignty, sometimes regally exercised. It also, of course, creates affection and loyalty. The nature and temperament of the family itself also accounts for the militant indictments.

Anyone even slightly acquainted with the history of the Christian Reformed Church knows that spirited controversy was never imported. Furthermore, while it may not be true that everyone over eighteen could split a hair 'twixt South and Southwest side, there

175

were many who tried and not a few that could. This church, never composed of shovel-handed, mindless clodhoppers, always contained many formally uneducated but highly intelligent laymen, who, together with the clergy, like debating fine points of doctrine. The Christian Reformed Church began in controversy, almost always has a controversial report to relegate to appropriate committees at Synod, and, wholly apart from the high issues involved, seems to enjoy the debates themselves. Some of the controversies, which we call *cases,* have been devoted to very subtle matters and have been argued with nimbleness and passion in the councils and papers of the church, sometimes, I fear, for victory as well as the truth. Calvin College, born into and partly of this temper, always living in its presence, and highly allergic to it by the nature of education itself, has not only reflected this controversial spirit but contributed to it.

The major precipitates of the war of words at and about Calvin College have been the college publications: *Chimes, The Literary Review,* and *Dialog;* the magazines to which the faculty have steadily contributed: *The Calvin Forum, The Reformed Journal,* and *The Torch and Trumpet,* now *The Outlook;* the lectures by the faculty in and out of the classroom, imported lecturers, entertainment, and student, faculty, and administrative action. The issue at stake is the limits of academic freedom in the light of the clearly stated ideals of the college. This issue concerns the heart of a college, and some account, though necessarily sketchy and somewhat impressionistic, should be given in the history of Calvin College. All these media at one time or another have provoked strong reaction by the constituency, a term often *falsely* identified with ungenerous and repressive narrow-mindedness.

The perennial context of the more specific criticism of the college to be discussed in this chapter is well exemplified by the early attacks in *The Witness* in 1921 by the Reverend Mr. H. J. Kuiper, for many years editor of *The Banner* and a singularly devoted critic of the college. *The Witness* was established because "the dangers which threaten us make it imperative that we post watchmen on all sides." H. J. Kuiper was such a watchman and he never slept at his post. He says in the first article, "We love our Alma Mater, and *out of love* we want to point out her faults." The faults are not tiny. The administration is preoccupied with scholarship. The faculty is more interested in scholarly reputation than in developing a Reformed life-and-world view. The spiritual life of the college is weak in piety, and the college community tends to imitate the world. Here are the perennial criticisms: the disillusioned voice of the pietistic element in the church and the dissatisfaction of the conservatives in doctrine. In one way or another, these have been the basic and reiterated criticisms of the college.

The *Calvin College Chimes* appeared in January 1907. Its purpose, according to Editor Dick Muyskens, was to stimulate literary effort and to "faithfully reflect school life." He warns against "hypercriticism." All three came true. The first issue contained critical pieces on Ten Kate's "Schepping" and Gray's "Elegy in a Country Churchyard." The first subscription manager was Wm. B. Eerdmans, who over many years gave sturdy support to the literary activity at the college.

In 1926, Dean Rooks remarks of the *Chimes* in the *Semi-Centennial Volume:*

> Ever since its inception it has appeared regularly all these years at the homes of our students and is especially a welcome guest of all our alumni and alumnae. In brief it presents in one way the mentality and life of the students of Calvin College.

That *Chimes* has reflected the mentality of many of the students is unquestionable. That it was always a welcome guest in the homes of alumni is highly debatable. It was for two decades written in Dutch and English; then in English; then in various forms of English. It can boast of many brilliant editors. It has served as outlet and proving ground for the nationally known authors Peter De Vries, Frederick Feikema Manfred, and David De Jong, as well as for many able writers in various forms. To ignore its contributions to the life of the college would be to ignore history and to miss drama. *Chimes* has been over the years an uncensored publication, to some observers a regrettably uncensored one. The various editors have expressed themselves clearly and sometimes stridently on their notions of the fundamental function of the paper. One of the most interesting and representative statements is that of Cornelius Van Til in January 1921. "*Chimes,*" says Van Til, "is the expression of the soul of the student." He then defines the nature and the limits of this expression:

> Let it not be inferred, however, that Calvin students speak timidly and without conviction. Nothing could be further from the truth or more remote from the ideal.

Van Til goes on to say, "Human authority, what is it? Every individual must stand or fall by himself." Consequently, the Reformed

student has an obligation to speak unflinchingly even in the face
of disapproval by his superiors. He must not fear antagonizing the
faculty or the Board. Van Til thinks both are far too "big-minded"
to feel offended at such action. Even if they are, however, the student with backbone will gladly risk such offense. He urges *Chimes*
to speak with fit modesty and unreserved conviction. C. Van Til and
his associates did not shirk their duty in 1921: later editors have on
occasion dropped even the pretense of modesty. Almost all have felt
with an editorialist in April 1928 that "we are sure that our school
will profit when *Chimes* gives vent to current thought."

During the first decades *Chimes* devoted itself largely to editorials, reflective essays, belated news, and literary efforts in poetry
and the short story. The editorial tone was friendly even when
critical. The subject matter was largely academic and ecclesiastical.
The writers did not then take on the United States and the rest of
the world. The paper was supported by advertisements and voluntary subscriptions, for which the staff had to hustle. *Chimes* in these
years had no painlessly available budget to be imperially spent. In
1930, Peter De Vries became editor, and for half a year the future
took over. The format became a bi-weekly newspaper with the style
racy.

De Vries was a highly articulate orator and writer, dedicated to
"open-minded statements." A typically "open-minded statement"
concerns his reaction to the repudiation by the Board of a Student
Council proposal:

> Now that our frail hopes have been championed before that au-
> gust assembly which pursues its agenda between huge draughts
> of Java and stern circumnavigation around the perimeters of
> doughnuts, and now that they have been duly blasted to atoms
> of smithereens by the roaring artillery of mustered dogma and
> by the noise of theological shrapnel, the student leaders of Cal-
> vin College can proceed on the perennial course of competitive
> begging. The student organization fee has been pigeon-holed by
> a very pious or very lazy Curatorium as a "violation of Chris-
> tian liberty."

At the end of the semester De Vries resigned, presumably because of
nervous exhaustion. He had for a few months, however, prefigured
the future in format and editorial exuberance. The Depression reduced the *Chimes* once more to a monthly, and it was not until 1946
that it became the newspaper weekly we have had since that date.

In 1916, Rector Heyns of the seminary reported to the Board that it was necessary to exercise a "light censure," and in 1925 he reports the appearance of an offensive piece in *Chimes,* which, although written by a college student, demanded seminary action because the editor was a pre-seminary student. But during its first quarter century *Chimes* caused little alarm. This favorable student spirit was largely due to a sturdy student devotion to first editor D. H. Muyskens' ideal that *Chimes* reflect loyalty to Calvinistic tenets. However, in the late twenties and thirties the solemn sense of the antithesis weakened, and the full impact of the dissolving twenties strengthened. A more critical, even defiant, spirit arose, to rise and fall over the years till it reached a temporary crescendo in the late sixties.

An editorial called "The Mind of Youth" appeared in March 1934, claiming that a large group of Calvin students "has wandered far afield intellectually and has become frankly hopeless of adjusting itself to the church." An even larger group is "repelled by certain things within the church," and a larger group still, though not intellectually or spiritually adrift, is "in its actual living largely unaffected by church influence." The cause, the writer asserts, does not lie in any "very special wickedness of modern youth"; rather, "the church itself is largely responsible for the fatal loss of its young people." What especially irritates these sensitive plants is the otherworldliness in the church and a "petty and highly offensive type of legalism." The church is too defensive, uncreative, traditional. It should respond happily to the idealism and creativity of youth. Here already in 1934 you have the basic patterns of 1968: the slanted picture of grim-faced Puritans patrolling the lives and bottling up innocent, idealistic, and creative youth. Such sentiments in 1934 greatly irritated some of the faculty, enraged some members of the Board, and helped initiate the Committee of Ten and its investigation of the College. No issue of *Chimes* was safely confined to Calvin College.

I do not mean to suggest that the editorializing was characteristic of *Chimes.* In this chapter I am dealing only with writings that brought Calvin under criticism. As a matter of fact *Chimes* has often contributed to the intellectual and spiritual growth of the college, and many of its writers were profoundly interested in fusing faith and learning. The fifties were especially significant in this respect, and writers like Neal Rensenbrink, Rod Jellema, Ron Jager, Nick Wolterstorff, Connie Ter Maat, and Nelvin Vos were highly gifted contributors to such an endeavor. Norman Tanis, in an editorial in the 1950's, said, "It is our duty to assert, refine, and strengthen Calvinism," and this they did.

Student literary publications were augmented in the fifties by *The Literary Review,* and in the sixties by *Dialog,* a student-faculty publication, and by the Fine Arts Anthology, now *Daedalus,* which included original photographs, musical compositions, and paintings. In 1955 an issue of *The Literary Review* was confiscated because it dealt with the life of a prostitute in a way the authorities considered a clear violation of its literary standards. A vocal student later complained that these standards were neither literary nor moral "but what would be offensive to the supporters of the college," who presumably had no sense of either. Minor crises flowed and ebbed as students gave "vent to current thought," reaching crests in 1968-70.

The *Chimes* of 1967-68 was editorially dedicated to diminished paternalism at the college, sharply independent opinions, fractional and frictional worry about the constituency, and impatience with "waiting for things to happen." The college community was advised, "Don't blow your cool, blow your mind." Blow it they did on Vietnam, race questions, politics, economics, and tradition. The *Chimes* of that school year was edited by superlatively gifted students, mesmerized by their own importance, and afflicted by subjectivity and tactlessness. Despite an abundance of talent, journalistic flair, and fresh ideas, they "blew" the paper as well as their minds. *Chimes* printed erroneous data, engaged in irresponsible attacks on the authorities, pursued personal vendettas under the banner of academic freedom. When the editor persisted in this course, after being warned of the lack of "Christian perspectives and Christian charity," the president, unanimously supported by the Executive Committee of the Student Council and the entire Publication Committee, asked the editor to resign. Later somebody stole the bound copies of the 1967-68 *Chimes* from the library.

In May 1970 the *Chimes* staff published a parody of *The Banner,* the official paper of the Christian Reformed Church, which though often spottily read, is held in high repute by the vast majority of the members of this church. This parody, a masterpiece of overkill, galvanized a massive voltage of protest that hit the college with searing impact. In his report to the Board of Trustees, President Spoelhof says, "In my twenty years as President of Calvin College, no one college incident touched off a greater storm than did the production of the student spoof last May. . . . Never has my mail been heavier." In the June 19 issue of *The Banner*, Editor Vander Ploeg, who had over several previous years been attacked by *Chimes* for his "editorial narrow-mindedness" and his "dangerous mode of thinking," replied with a four-page editorial, "Do We Just Laugh This Off?" After a fair-minded reader has admitted the incontestable ingenuity and literary skill in the parody, and after he allows for the legitimacy of exaggeration in satire, he will still, I think, find much that is unjustified and tasteless. The demolition of inept but sincere and unpretentious poetry, the deflation of sensible articles to a parade of inanities, even the grotesque and sometimes salacious reworking of advertisements marked no high moment in satiric art. In view of the unjustifiable pain it caused, I think the satirical ingenuity in *The Bananer* was badly misapplied. The Reverend Mr. Vander Ploeg was, however, utterly unable to conceive of the parody as rising out of anything but malice, or of excusing youthful indiscretion. He says, "The whole thing is deplorable, a disgrace to Calvin College, and at times nothing less than blasphemy," and asks "Who are the perverted minds that dreamed up this devil's brew?" Knowing that some people will say "I am overreacting to this thing," he goes on to excoriate the issue in detail. He states that he is unsatisfied with mild rebukes and apologies that have later occurred. Letters to *The Banner* threatened to preempt the magazine, so they were no longer printed. The faculty drew up a resolution stating that "We certainly do *not* condone the publication of the parody, and we express our regrets to any who are personally offended and angered by its contents." The Board drew up a set of guidelines for future parodies, thereby insuring intramural and responsible limits.

Many supporters of Calvin think the college should turn out manifestly Christian artists and turn off those who are not. After all, they say, the college guidelines are abundantly clear in catalog after catalog. Furthermore, the Publication Committee in 1966 states the matter precisely by insisting that school publications "must reflect a living and thoughtful Reformed perspective on life" and that "all student writing shall be consistent with a loyalty to Scripture." If the words mean what they say, they at the very least mean that the spirit and moral stance of the work should not be hostile to the Reformed commitment. I share these ideals, but would immediately rule out censorship as a way to achieve them. Censorship stifles creativity, impairs the educational process, and violates the dignity of all involved. Education implies a sympathetic patterning of the mind and room for hypothesis and experimentation which, it is hoped, will produce and strengthen commitment to Christian perspectives. Furthermore, through a clear statement of principles, the appointment of spiritually sensitive students and faculty members to the proper committees, the careful scrutiny of prospective editors, a genuine effort is made to secure responsible writing and artistic achievement. Such a process is a calculated risk. If an editor or artist clearly violates the ideals of the college he will be rebuked; if he persists, the committee should remove him, even if the artist then attempts, in the words of one of them, to "reveal them to the world for the fools they will show themselves to be."

Calvin College has always shown a strong interest in the creative talents of its students; it has liberally supported the arts in publication, performance, and exhibit. Faculty members in the departments most directly involved—Art, English, Music, and Speech—have selflessly given countless hours of encouragement and advice. They have emphasized perspectives congenial to the ideals of the college. Unfortunately, some students regard such suggestion as an encumbrance. The artistic student is often hypersensitive and hypercritical. He wants to beat his own thought and rhythm out. Frequently mistaking sensibility for insight and rebellion for wisdom when he bursts upon the scene long-haired and loud-mouthed, he strikes some supporters of Calvin as something demonic. When the work he produces is at variance with the professed ideals of the college, he becomes a problem not only in public relations but in spiritual loyalties. The college has a right to insist upon its religious commitments. This student is, we should remember, a product of the very constituency whom we seek to serve. He attended our schools and our churches, and his rebellious attitudes should be sympathetically understood as well as corrected if possible. Instant and angry repudiation is not the answer. Yet I think President Spoelhof is wholly correct when he said in an interview:

> . . . if that student would stay only on the condition that we would change the mould of the college or the purpose of the institution, I would say—regret it or not, that student should really be elsewhere.

Calvin is committed to giving Christ preeminence in all things: work that imperils that ideal cannot be tolerated. I think it is worthwhile to remember a comment of the poet and critic Allen Tate: "Poetry does not dispense with tradition; it probes the deficiencies of a tradition. But it must have a tradition to probe." However incorrect one may view their probing, I think Calvin College has given its rebels a tough tradition to rebel against. They weren't slugging it out with styrofoam.

Although the writings of the faculty and the journals in which they published are not officially, except in the case of *The Calvin Forum,* part of the history of Calvin College, yet these writings often did reflect and affect college life and the community it served. There is an interesting pattern in the nature of the journals to which the faculty contributed. In 1919, *Religion and Culture,* edited by the Reverend Mr. E. J. Tuuk, appeared. Its main objectives were "to publish essays with some scientific merit and productions of some literary value," and to serve as a "clearing house for the best thought of all our educated men and women, holding to the Reformed view of God and the world." To this magazine a number of Calvin's faculty contributed—in the case of Henry Van Andel, voluminously. This journal sought to affect the world, to develop the faith; it tried to be an American periodical, Reformed but not ecclesiastical. In 1919, *The Witness* appeared. Its main objective was safeguarding doctrinal purity. Although it claimed no purpose of rebutting "liberal" tendencies in *Religion and Culture,* it was certainly watching. *Religion and Culture* on the other hand magnanimously stated, "We welcome new light from whatever quarter it may come." By 1925 both had suspended publication; but the temper of each magazine reappeared in the almost simultaneous publication of *The Reformed Journal* and *The Torch and Trumpet* in 1951.

The Calvin Forum, first published in 1935, was specifically a college and seminary publication, subsidized by the Board. In his opening editorial, Dr. Clarence Bouma proposed a heady program:

> It is to be devoted to the helpful discussion of subjects in the realms of Religion and Theology, History and Philosophy, Natural Science and Medicine, Sociology and Economics, Political Science and International Law, Psychology and Education, Literature and Art.

Although he forgot Philately and Heraldry, it is an impressive list, and worthy of the memory of Professor Egbert Boer, although now there was more than one man available to do the job. Dr. Bouma emphasized the importance of being "progressive and open-minded" as well as being "loyal to the spiritual heritage of our group." In his editorship, which he carried on while teaching full time in the seminary, he literally spent himself in writing provocative editorials, in securing good copy, often from reluctant colleagues, and in obtaining interesting correspondence from around the world. His courageous utterances, especially on economic and social issues, angered conservative readers. Neither he nor his adversaries were devoted to gentleness, and the ensuing rhetoric was often acidulous. Like Emily Dickinson, they often "dealt their pretty words like blades."

In 1951, after editing *The Calvin Forum* with distinction for fifteen years, Dr. Bouma suffered a nervous breakdown. Six months later Dr. Cecil De Boer of the Department of Philosophy became its editor. He responded to the new task with unexpected vigor, superlative journalistic skill, obvious zest, and blunt honesty until his shocking death in 1956.

Cecil De Boer was a memorable editor. Marked by an analytical and cutting mind, master of a honed and lucid prose, impatient with dulness or timidity, he did not hesitate to engage in critical evaluation. Having taught philosophy for years at the University of Arkansas and then for some years at the University of Idaho, he brought to his writing a perceptive awareness of the intellectual life in American universities. He had also a thorough knowledge of the Reformed tradition, and the scholarly patience to read contemporary Dutch philosophy as well as the nerve to attack it. His writings in *The Calvin Forum,* as Dr. Zylstra says in his preface to *Responsible Protestantism,* a collection of De Boer's writings edited by Zylstra, constitute an "impressively honest, earned and informed interpretation of faith and life." De Boer spoke without fear and attacked with obvious relish the opinions of Professor Cornelius Van Til of Westminster Seminary and Professor Herman Dooyeweerd of the Free University of Amsterdam. Angry responses came from H. J. Kuiper as well as from others. Whether one agreed with De Boer or not, one could hardly be unimpressed by his quality of mind or the prose in which it was expressed.

De Boer's unexpected death at fifty-seven impoverished his friends, the college, the church he served, and *The Calvin Forum,* which was unable to survive his demise. Laconic, frank, witty, and tender-hearted beneath his occasional rough manner and always burly appearance, he combined a deep, warm faith with unusual philosophical talent. He was a delightful companion whether in the home, in the faculty room, or on the golf course. His remarks were often sharply vivid and delivered with Johnsonian certitude. He could be erratic and sometimes supercilious. One morning he left school early, muttering, "I have had enough of mediocrity for one day." He could cut people down, but only those he thought needed it. Although he had suffered tragic loss in life and knew what loneliness was from the inside, he met both with faith, courage, and humor. Those who were privileged to know him well treasure his memory.

After De Boer died, the problem of finding a new editor proved insoluble. Despite the quality of the magazine, subscriptions dwindled alarmingly. Evidently its open point of view and semi-scholarly character irritated or discouraged readers, and no one wished to pilot it into oblivion. The last issue appeared in February 1956, and the Board reimbursed subscribers for unexpired subscriptions. It succumbed not of pointlessness but indifference.

After World War II political issues began to arouse faculty comment and a "Pink Menace" was feared to exist at Calvin. In some cases, worried critics of the college saw red. I remember a former high school student of mine asserting in all seriousness that when the Soviet tanks would rumble into Grand Rapids, Professor Stob of the Seminary would be riding on one of them. Professor Lester De Koster would be directing the squadron. He had, of course, read none of De Koster's attacks on Communism. De Koster had in *The Banner* of August 18, 1950, attacked the National Association of Evangelicals for recommending the rabidly right-wing book *The Road Ahead,* by John T. Flynn. The Christian Reformed Church, then a member of the association, had supported the recommendation. H. J. Kuiper, Editor of *The Banner,* who had in the early thirties attacked Dr. Henry Ryskamp for his allegedly socialistic views, rushed to the defense of the good old ways and blasted De Koster's article. Kuiper found Flynn's book authentic and completely convincing. He found De Koster's review worrisome and smelled a socialist in the rubbish. De Koster replied by denying all socialist tendencies and affirming his devotion to "private property, private enterprise, and human freedom, all under law." Kuiper then claimed he saw a mile-high drift to socialism in the country and was amazed that De Koster didn't.

Then, in *The Banner* of August 26, 1950, eighteen college and seminary professors published a signed reaction to Kuiper's editorial on Flynn, in which they said among other things:

> We make this report lest it be generally understood in the Reformed community and elsewhere that the Flynn line of thought is the Reformed line of contemporary economic-political thought.

Reverend Mr. Kuiper replied with massive irony. He knows, he says, sardonically, how highly our people view the learning at Calvin College and Seminary, "but who is ready to agree with their utterance merely because they are Professors at our school and in number eighteen?" He does not doubt they made a careful study of the Reformed writers on these matters, a remarkable feat since most of them work in "altogether different fields of study and research." He asks for more benefits from their research.

The professors replied with tallying tartness. They affirmed themselves to be squarely in the economic and political traditions of Calvin, Van Prinsterer, Kuyper, and other Reformed leaders. They would share their learning in appropriate places and times, but they concluded "that in view of your kind of editorial writing and comment, no further statement in *The Banner* can be fruitful."

Kuiper was, however, unsatisfied by this conclusion of the affair and was determined to purge the college and seminary of undesirable ideas and persons. He was alarmed that Calvin was losing her distinctiveness and circulated a petition throughout the country pleading for signatures so that an impressive concern might be submitted to the Synod of 1952. He was intent upon capitalizing on the alarm about Calvin in the church and the sentiment that "some heads must roll." The *Petition* expressed grave fears that the professional guidance of certain teachers at Calvin "along Reformed lines" was inept or nonexistent, that there "is no pronounced spiritual atmosphere in our college," that there is "an emphasis in the English Department which we believe to be unwholesome and deleterious." Furthermore, some (no number is given) maintain there is no proper integration of faith and learning. Synod is, therefore, urged "to purify the college."

These undocumented assertions, founded on scattered student impressions, were signed by one hundred and forty-seven persons, most of whom could not have had the foggiest idea of what they were talking about. The Reverend Mr. H. J. Kuiper must have been disappointed in the small number of signatures. One hundred and forty-seven members out of 150,000 wasn't very alarming. The Synod of 1952 refused to accept the petition and "greatly deplored" the manner in which the grievances were brought.

H. J. Kuiper was not the only one submitting petitions in the early fifties or the only one to be criticized for "the manner in which the grievances were brought." There were seven college students, often referred to as "the sacred seven," who also had grievances to bring. Here I remind you that it is always open season on professors.

At Calvin none of us has had to publish or perish, but we have all had to reveal ourselves in teaching. In so doing we all face criticism whether aroused by severe discipline, poor grades, abrasive personality, skipping classes, inveterate dulness, inertia, pedagogical ineptness, jarring points of view, or even mannerisms. In the twenties, thirties, and forties such criticism was largely subterranean. In print, portraits of professors dripped with eulogy. Students even gave farewell banquets to retiring professors, who, after being sumptuously lauded, responded with carefully rehearsed bewilderment. This kind of attention evaporated in the fifties. In the sixties, evaluation sheets to be "carefully checked" were distributed to students. The results were designed to improve the teaching at Calvin College. And this they did. Dulness was eradicated, innovation burgeoned everywhere, severity melted into compassion, abrasive personalities became beatific, animated discussions crackled in the classrooms, wit enlivened the comma fault, and Reformed perspectives were applied as never before. The teachers whom the sacred seven attacked had, however, had no such help.

In May of 1951 these seven students brought a manuscript of fifteen pages to the Board of Trustees without consulting either Dean Ryskamp or President Schultze or apprizing any of the six faculty members concerned, who found copies of the grievances already delivered to the Board in their mailboxes on a sunny Friday morning. Improperly handled, great damage could have been done; wisely handled as it was by President Schultze and President Spoelhof and the Discipline Committee of the college, the protest left little more than unpleasant memories.

The grievances were formulated because the plaintiffs feared "that man was being enthroned at Calvin College instead of God." The document, rising out of "mingled emotions of love, sorrow, and firm convictions," then lists errors in faith and practice exemplified by the teaching of six members of the faculty: three from the Department of English and one each from the Departments of Philosophy, Sociology, and Education. The charges consist largely of unfounded and poorly phrased allegations based on cloudy misinterpretations of classroom comments wrenched out of context. Here are random, representative, and uncorrected statements.

In one class the professor questioned the validity and propriety of our forefathers in condemning all non-Christian literature and allowing only Christian literature to be read by their children.

But some professors insist that every literary product has some good.

The teaching profession was degraded by emotional and unnecessary description of the low salaries and heavy burdens borne by Christian School teachers.

In another of the English classes, a student related how he had been denied permission to withdraw a certain book from the library [*Lust For Life,* a biography of Van Gogh]. This book had been branded by one of the professors as unfit for students to read. Therefore the librarian refused to grant him the book. When this student concluded relating his experience the students in the class burst forth into laughter and the professor joined them. Thus the fact that there are books which are unfit for human consumption is ridiculed even by our professors.

For instance, when a student answered that he had learned from Ancient Philosophy that the pagan was unable to arrive at truth without the Word, the position of the student was made to appear absurd.

Calvinism is a system of law and order. However professor [X] seldom come to class less than ten minutes after the class period has begun. In one class of which many of us are members there are more than forty-five students. In one semester alone and in only this *one* class he wastes considerable more than 300 hours of the student's time.

The only course in education that is a requirement for theological students is wholly negative. Nothing positive is given.

[The Professor] in discussing birth control uses subtle arguments and quasi-objective arguments whereby the God-given mandate to replenish the earth is ridiculed. . . . Or again, after quoting, "Happy is the man who has his quiver full of them (i.e. children)," Prof. [X] will ask what represents a full quiver. . . . Also the case of a man with 22 children, who is on relief, is ridiculed as an example of what happens when anyone takes God's commands too seriously.

Furthermore, in some cases "the words spoken as such are often not to be criticized, but the tonal inflections [speak] more forcibly than the meaning of the words."

The lengthy tirade concludes with a section called "In General" in which the students inform the Board exactly how teaching should be conducted at Calvin College, how *The Literary Review* should be created and judged, how recommendations should be written for the Placement Bureau, and how the college atmosphere should be altered. In conclusion, the paper states that it is emphasizing only "unsound teachings" not "inefficiencies," of which there are many.

The students were doubtless sincere as well as arrogant and unfair. The professors could doubtless have been clearer and duller. The method of criticism was potentially sinister and universally condemned by the faculty. The Board, however, took the matter very seriously because of the widespread suspicion and doubt the activities of the Reverend Mr. H. J. Kuiper had engendered. It appointed a committee of five who spent "nine full days . . . . in committee meetings alone, in which [they] struggled to come to some satisfactory conclusion." They met with the professors and the Discipline Committee and held four sessions with the seven students. They had a perplexing and immensely difficult task. The professors described the charges as "lying, preposterous, irresponsible, bungling philosophy of aesthetics, narrow preconceived notions." They all decried the illegality of the procedure. The Discipline Committee protested the method of procedure. Furthermore, the Board knew that the students completely lacked the support of their classmates. The Committee seemed to have to choose between falsification or stupidity on the one hand or total inability to communicate on the other. The latter was a particularly hard choice because of the general reputation of the professors under attack. The Committee itself was totally without malice and acted with fairness and courtesy at all times. Since they had no wish to discipline either party, they recommended the creation of a larger committee to conduct a much more intensive investigation. But then something else happened.

In May of 1952, Dr. Cornelius Van Til, who long ago in the *Chimes* of January 1921 said:

> Let it not be inferred, however, that Calvin students speak timidly and without conviction. Nothing could be further from the truth or more remote from the ideal.

and who was currently serving as visiting Professor of Apologetics at the Calvin Seminary engaged in public debate with Dr. William Masselink in the crowded little chapel of the Hekman Memorial Seminary Building. Dr. Masselink with evangelistic fervor asserted that Dr. Van Til was denying the doctrine of common grace as properly interpreted by Bavinck, Kuyper, and Hepp. The room tingled with tension as Dr. Van Til, obviously aroused, repudiated this tradition and then said that if Calvin were to follow it, "We might as well blow up the Science Building with an atom bomb." Many were greatly angered by this hyperbole and the anger was apparent. In *The Christian Reformed Church and Her Schools,* Dr. George Stob notes that "when the tape recording of the debate was played again in Ripon, California, the tape was oddly broken at that particular point." In a later book Dr. Van Til retracted the hyperbole but not the sentiment behind it. Some of his followers actively pressed the sentiments in classroom and public statements.

By this time there was a good deal to be alarmed about. Eighteen professors had dared publicly to rebuke the prestigious editor of *The Banner,* Professor De Koster was allegedly sowing socialistic seed, the Van Tilians were quick to find fault, a *Petition* of protest was being circulated throughout the church, and six professors were accused of inadequate integration of faith and learning as well as of "inefficiencies . . . of which there are many." As the Board meeting approached, President Spoelhof, who had succeeded President Schultze, initiated strong counter action. A document signed by all the faculty was submitted to the Board and received with "keen appreciation." In the document the faculty reaffirmed its traditional loyalties: "the absolute Lordship of Christ," the authority of Scripture, the historic Reformed creeds, and belief in the reality of the antithesis. The faculty also emphasized the immensely difficult task of integration. The Board in turn submitted the document to Synod. There was some sense of mortification on the part of the faculty, since they felt that they had never lapsed in loyalty to these affirmations and to repeat them seemed superfluous. However, the issuance of the document and Board approval of faculty recommendations for proper procedures in registering complaints cleared the air. Never since has the faculty experienced such sustained and widespread criticism. Attacks of various kinds did not cease, but they were courteously and wisely handled by President Spoelhof.

The atmosphere of mistrust did not evaporate immediately. In September of 1952, Dr. Henry Stob published "A Note to a College Freshman" in *The Reformed Journal.* With grace and precision, he defines the mind a student should develop during his college career. The student's mind, or spiritual center, should transcend the merely subjective. It should be enriched by the universal human mind as expressed in cultural monuments. The Christian student, however, must transcend this mind also and "attain the mind of Christ," which, indeed, strictly speaking one cannot attain at all since it is God's gift. Without this gift "no man is educated, just as without it no man is saved." The goal of education is "to be shaped by the Word and Spirit and the whole of God's creation into conformity to the mind of Christ." I thought it a fine piece and recommended it to my classes. The article, however, received stiff criticism. The president of the seminary, the Reverend Mr. R. B. Kuiper, took an active interest in it and its proper rebuttal. When Dr. Stob's reappointment came up, "the substance of an article recently written by him in *The Reformed Journal*" was submitted in evidence for unfavorable action. Such action never occurred.

Although attacks similar to those described above never recurred, there were from time to time sabre-rattling students armed with omniscient ideologies who entered the classroom with a mission and a missile. Convinced of their possession of both insight and rectitude, they minimized the drudgery of learning and concentrated on principles of interpretation, which in the case of one group had to be accepted even to experience learning itself. There were in my experience three such groups. One group called themselves Van Tilians. They often attempted to turn class discussion into class instruction. They were openly supported by a zesty professor who would criticize his colleagues in class by name. Wearying of their tactics, I had them dictate statements in class which expressed their basic positions. I told them I was taking them to R. B. Kuiper, then president of the seminary a few yards away, to see whether the statements were both Van Tilian and Reformed, a matter I doubted. I was glad to report to the next meeting of the class that he said the statements were not Reformed and that he did not agree with them. Some years later a group appeared devoted to the language and theory of the philosophy of the Law-Idea, a system of thought primarily associated with Professor Dooyeweerd of the Free University, Dr. Runner of Calvin College, and the AACS in Canada. Some of them asserted in class and out that the Reformed positions most of the faculty taught were not even Christian. In 1971 at a symposium on chapel in which I participated, a particularly bright young lady gave a sassy speech identifying all who did not subscribe to this position as unchristian; she was an extremist no doubt, but typically militant. In the late sixties a group, not technically philosophers but rather a loosely knit group of self-appointed geniuses inclined to behavioristic psychology, blasted traditional Reformed positions in class and in

Chimes. These groups were abrasive and impolite, but they had the courage of their convictions. They evaluated you by open comment. Though ill at ease with them all, I respected them for their candor.

In the rather waspish little debate with the Reverend Mr. H. J. Kuiper, the eighteen professors had promised to reply at the proper time and place. One medium in which some of them did so was *The Reformed Journal,* first published in March 1951. The magazine attempted to speak out of Reformed perspectives not "only on ecclesiastical matters but as well on other things that belong to the scope of Christian life and thought." In April of the same year, *The Torch and Trumpet* appeared, also dedicated to a similarly high ideal and a modest circulation. Some people wondered why *The Torch and Trumpet* appeared on the heels of *The Reformed Journal,* but the sponsors disclaimed any plot or controversial intent, although the latter was soon apparent. Professor Henry Van Til said of *The Torch and Trumpet,* "Its purpose is not to oppose other journals but to complement them." The emphases in the magazines have been decidedly different, but both have been frank and outspoken, and even in disagreement both have illuminated different outlooks in the church. During its existence of nearly a quarter century, *The Reformed Journal* has spoken creatively and vigorously on many matters that concern the Christian life in the world. In 1957 its readers were saddened by the death of Henry Zylstra, remembered elsewhere in this book, who had contributed heavily towards its excellence.

Articles published in *The Reformed Journal* have often provoked counter-attack but none so vehement and with such dramatic consequences as that occasioned by a "Special Supplement on the Far Right" in January 1965, which was acidly critical of Dr. McIntyre, the well-known critic of communism. McIntyre responded to the supplement with his accustomed intensity over the radio and at a mass rally in the Civic Auditorium in Grand Rapids, Michigan. He flayed the six writers, the editor of *Chimes,* who had called him "Mac the Knife," and Calvin College, which tolerated their presence. He demanded public apology from the six writers, who replied, "What for?"

After speaking in the Civic Auditorium, where he deplored what the "college students are being taught in our beloved city of Grand Rapids," he was, in what was a truly magnanimous gesture, invited to speak at the Calvin Chapel to the faculty and students. The audience jammed the chapel and flowed over into the hall and contained a sizable number of McIntyre's zealous supporters. He was cordially introduced by President Spoelhof and the two engaged in a pleasant interchange of wit. The Reverend Mr. McIntyre spoke with animation and considerable stridency, emphatically denying that he had ever called Calvin a "hot bed of socialism." Using a passage from the Psalms as Biblical warrant, he recommended individualism and free enterprise as not only thoroughly Biblical but as the only hope for America. There were no untoward incidents. At the end of McIntyre's blazing address, President Spoelhof, in a fine tactical move, had the audience sing the "Alma Mater." Then Dr. McIntyre marched from the chapel out to his car, rigidly flanked by his lieutenants. I watched him closely as he marched brusquely down the walk, but his face showed neither chagrin nor triumph. He had been courteously treated at every point, and his visit stimulated a certain good will even in the face of markedly hostile differences of opinion.

This chapter has concerned itself with attacks in and about words. Other means of expression at Calvin have aroused similar hostility. Paintings and photographs, dramatic and musical productions, and movies shown by the Film Council have all been condemned. I have chosen to deal with written and spoken words because they can be quoted. Whatever the media employed, the fundamental issues are identical. How does their use realize or imperil the ideals of Calvin College?

Calvin College, as its history convincingly proves, has always enjoyed enormous support from its constituency. It has also, as this chapter shows, experienced from the same source a unique surveillance and critical assessment. I see no prospect of a diminution of either, unless either changes radically. As long as Calvin is supported by a constituency composed of pietistic elements who suspect learning, traditionalists who insist upon doctrinal purity, and Kuyperians of one kind or another, who emphasize creative development and cultural engagement, and as long as the college stresses loyalty to Reformed perspectives, there will be tension about what the "absolute Lordship of Christ" implies in an educational institution. There will be pietists who echo or rephrase a statement submitted to Synod in 1952:

> Why is it, for example, that the important Scriptural truth of the necessity of separation from the evil world is so foreign or obnoxious to many of the students?

There will be those who ask the perennial question, "Is Calvin College losing its distinctiveness?" and they mean by distinctiveness doctrinal purity. There will be those who like B. K. Kuiper in 1918 will say, "If one is oh so very Reformed, but not scholarly, then as a *professor* he is worth exactly *nothing*," and by "scholarly" Kuiper meant creative development of Reformed principles.

These are our voices; they are rooted in the Reformed tradition, and they are Christian. We need them. We need to be reminded that our highest loyalties are not to the kingdoms of this world, that true Christianity is grounded in doctrinal purity, and that we must be a light and salt in our world. These voices may and do produce tension and frustration. The angry telephone calls, the critical, even abusive, letters, the unfair editorials, the guerrilla attacks occasionally employed should be met with calm, firm, and open response. Relying on the profound loyalty of a host of supporters, the Calvin community will with God's grace attempt to fulfill the doubly difficult task of mastery of knowledge and its illumination through Reformed perspectives.

INDEX OF PERSONS